J. Franklin Jameson:
A Tribute

FOURTEEN CONTRIBUTORS

Edited by

Ruth Anna Fisher

William Lloyd Fox

THE CATHOLIC UNIVERSITY OF AMERICA PRESS
Washington, D.C. 20017

The American Historical Association participates in the publication of this volume under the terms of the will of Frank Maloy Anderson. Professor Anderson specified that a portion of his bequest to the Association be used 'to foster research with respect to the founders of The American Historical Association.'

Publication of this book has also been aided by a grant from The American Catholic Historical Association.

Library of Congress Catalog Number: 65-16326

TABLE OF CONTENTS

INTRODUCTION

To awaken an interest in the memory and achievements of John Franklin Jameson, which the twenty-seven years since his death have naturally diminished, we have collected these essays. They are in no way meant to be a biography, only a reminder of a great scholar and a great man.

Our sources for arousing this interest are limited to Dr. Jameson's few contemporaries still living, those younger historians whose mentor and helper he was but who could have known him only slightly, and also the undertakings of other historians who have researched and reported on some of those imaginative projects of his which greatly furthered interest and activities in the field of American History.

In the first group is Waldo Gifford Leland, a graduate student of Dr. Jameson at Brown University and later a member of his staff in the Department of Historical Research of the Carnegie Institution of Washington. This put him in the unique position of being able to write authoritatively of one of Dr. Jameson's most favored projects, the National Historical Publications Commission.

As either readers in or members of the staff of the Manuscript Division of the Library of Congress, we obtained the following contributors: Professor Mary R. Dearing, Montgomery Junior College; Miss Ruth Anna Fisher, a co-editor of this volume; Dr. Curtis W. Garrison, the Office of the U. S. Army Supply and Maintenance Command; Professor emeritus Dumas Malone, University of Virginia;

Donald H. Mugridge, Library of Congress; and Dr. Allan Nevins, Huntington Library and Gallery of Art.

Two other contributors knew Dr. Jameson by their association with the Library of Congress but not as members of his staff: Verner W. Clapp, Council on Library Resources, Inc.; and David C. Mearns, Library of Congress.

Some of the contributors knew Dr. Jameson slightly or not at all but had special knowledge of several of his enterprises: The Right Reverend John Tracy Ellis, University of San Francisco; Professor William Lloyd Fox, Montgomery Junior College, a co-editor of this book; Professor Boyd C. Shafer, Macalaster College; Fred Shelley, Library of Congress; and Dr. John K. Wright, Librarian emeritus, American Geographical Society of New York.

Along with our contributors we wish to give special thanks to The American Catholic Historical Association and The American Historical Association for their most generous financial help, and to the following persons for various assistance in reading our manuscripts, in criticizing and suggesting improvements in our plans, and in typing the final draft of the book: Mrs. G. Philip Bauer, Carnegie Institution of Washington; Miss Burney Bennett, University of Michigan; Dr. Lester K. Born, Library of Congress; Judge and Mrs. Henry W. Edgerton; Mrs. Hanna S. Fields, Montgomery Junior College; Professor John J. Finan, The American University; Mrs. William Lloyd Fox; Miss Patricia M. Fox, _The American Historical Review;_ Professor Wood Gray, The George Washington University; Professor W. Stull Holt, University of Washington; Professor Harold D. Langley, The Catholic University of America; Ronald E. Latham, Public Record Office; Mrs. Clara LeGear, Library of Congress; Mr. and Mrs. Edgar Ansel Mowrer; and Reverend Peter J. Rahill, The Catholic University of America Press.

Lest we should be accused of bias in our unstinted admiration of Dr. Jameson, may we here add two estimates of him from other sources. One of them appeared in an unsigned

J. Franklin Jameson:
A Tribute

A Chronicle of John Franklin Jameson's Life

1859	Born on September 19, in Somerville, Massachusetts
1874	Graduated from Roxbury Latin School
1879	Received Bachelor's degree from Amherst College
1879-80	Taught History and Latin in Worcester (Mass.) High School
1882	Received the Ph.D. degree from The Johns Hopkins University (the first Ph.D. in history to be conferred by that university)
1882-88	Taught at The Johns Hopkins University
1884	A charter member of The American Historical Association
1888-1901	Professor of History, Brown University
1895	Became chairman of the Historical Manuscripts Commission of The American Historical Association and managing editor of *The American Historical Review*
1901-05	Professor and Chairman, Department of History, University of Chicago
1905-28	Director, Department of Historical Research, Carnegie Institution of Washington
1907	President, The American Historical Association; his presidential address: "The American Acta Sanctorum"
1926	Publication of *The American Revolution Considered as a Social Movement*
1928-37	Chief, Division of Manuscripts, Library of Congress, and first occupant of the Library's Chair of American History
1934	An Act to Establish a National Archives of the United States Government . . . (June 19), the fulfillment of a twenty-five-year campaign by Jameson (Three years later the National Archives building was completed.)
1937	Died on September 28 at his home in Washington, D. C.

tribute in *The American Historical Review* (January, 1938) a few months after his death:

> We shall not see his like again, if only because the circumstances under which his work was done will never recur. He had no predecessor, and he will have no successor.

Herbert Putnam, the distinguished Librarian of Congress, upon learning of Dr. Jameson's death, wrote:

> Many gain fame by the writing of history; he was content to aid them to gain it. His career was a long devotion to their service, and to the promotion of historical studies. In the latter, no American has by personal effort done so much, or to such practical purpose. He labored patiently and with remarkable sagacity in the construction of the necessary apparatus. He gave dignity to it. And he responded without stint to any particular request for his counsel, requiring no credential, nor any least recognition to himself.

Ruth Anna Fisher
William Lloyd Fox

A TRIBUTE

by Ruth Anna Fisher

For famous men praise is seldom lacking. Their character, background and achievements are chronicled in minute detail, an open book for all to read. Many things contribute to the publicity of their fame—their family, their deeds and sometimes the mere circumstances of the particular period in which they lived as, for instance, a time of revolution, war, economic expansion or even an awakened interest in learning and the arts. But are there not countless others with no such propitious background of time and events to whom equal praise is due? Their deeds may have been less spectacular and known only to a few. But these deeds, nevertheless, have made an impact in their own field which nothing can erase though their names may be long since forgotten.

Dr. J. Franklin Jameson is such a neglected scholar and man. As with his height of over six feet he towered over most of his fellowmen physically, his mental height was equally impressive and his New England courtesy outstandingly gracious and kindly. Yet the mention of his name now seldom evokes more than a lifted eyebrow as if to ask Who was he? and What did he do?

Yet Dr. Jameson's contributions to American historiography were remarkable. Many broke new ground. He assisted in founding The American Historical Association and its publication, *The American Historical Review*, among many other activities. And what must have given him

great happiness was the stimulus his efforts provided for
students of American history. Many of his imaginative suggestions, practical as they were, so far outstripped the thinking of his contemporaries as to lie dormant for several years.
It is then a matter of rejoicing among historians that his
idea of a center for advanced studies here in Washington,
with all the physical amenities necessary, should have been
broached in the presidential address, "A Modest Proposal
to Meet an Urgent Need," given by Dr. Julian P. Boyd at
the seventy-ninth annual meeting of The American Historical Association in 1964.

It seemed to me that this contribution was too great
and far too important to be allowed to pass without proper
recognition. I felt I was inadequate to perform the task.
But surely there were many historians who would be glad
to see that Dr. Jameson became a living rather than a dead
monument in the historical world. A small volume of essays
on the various aspects of his work edited by one of his
indebted colleagues seemed the perfect answer. This would
at least prepare the way for the much needed biography to
come later. In 1962 I then began writing certain historians
explaining my idea and asking what they thought of the
plan, and if they would be willing to undertake it. A long
wait for their replies followed. Since Dr. Jameson's colleagues were no longer young, there came letters applaud-
ing the idea which they thought long overdue but regretfully
declining the task because of illness or age. Determined
that the idea should not be stillborn and since no one seemed
available for the undertaking, I felt I must try myself.

Then providentially there came to my assistance Dr.
William Lloyd Fox who had become interested in Dr.
Jameson through the publication of his letters in *An Historian's World,* which Leo Stock and Elizabeth Donnan had
edited.

We accordingly made a list of persons who in any way
had been associated with some of Dr. Jameson's enterprises
and asked them for an essay for our proposed volume. The

response was wonderful. The key sentence in each reply was, "I should be much honored to be allowed to contribute to a volume in memory of Jameson." Writing an essay seemed a less arduous and responsible task than editing. Thus the story begins with a list of distinguished contributors.

My own meeting with Dr. Jameson was casual enough. As the year for which I had been given funds for study in London came to an end, I was in that unenviable situation with which students often have been too familiar— I had neither the money to return to America, which I did not want to do, nor to stay on in London, which I wanted very much to do. Anticipating such an event before I left America, a friend had given me Dr. Jameson's address at the Carnegie Institution of Washington. She thought as he was then engaged in having copies made of documents in British archives relating to American history he might find me some work which would enable me to stay in London until I was able to make other plans. Consequently, I wrote Dr. Jameson. In due time, to my surprise, I had a reply from London, for he was then himself working in the Public Record Office while on a short vacation. In answer to his letter I met him at that office and at once began working for him. Later I transferred to the Library of Congress a few years before he became Chief of its manuscript department. This made our association a continuous one from then until his death.

Over this period I naturally discovered much about Dr. Jameson. He was shy, inordinately so, so much in fact that when he first began to teach I learned he found it difficult to keep order, his shyness preventing a rapport between him and his students.

Shyness often produces curtness and sometimes even unintended rudeness. But Dr. Jameson's courtesy invariably overcame his shyness. I realized this early in our acquaintance. At the end of my first week of work with him we came out of the Public Record Office together and at its Chancery

Lane entrance parted. I had gone but a short distance when, on hearing my name called, turned to see Dr. Jameson coming towards me. Raising his hat as he came near he said, "I cannot let you go without thanking you for your very real help." I knew he had not forgotten that he had already thanked me most kindly.

However, this shyness often did prevent a warm friendship between him and many persons who would have enjoyed knowing him. These initial stages of frigidity were hard to overcome. To youth, frigidity is no obstacle. Like many young people I easily recognized and respected greatness: I was never overawed by it. Hence, those stages in our relationship which might have hindered further acquaintance were easily eliminated. It was this which made seem almost impossible to me the question of a learned history professor who sat at a table near where Dr. Jameson and I were lunching. "How can you talk so easily and freely with Dr. Jameson?" she asked. "He frightens me so I can hardly speak in his presence."

This reserve did nothing to prevent him from having an eye for a pretty girl nor from exacting high standards in the work required; nor when these standards were not met from making such caustic criticisms as to leave one limp and dazed. "There isn't a single person here whom I would have working for me for five minutes," he once said as he walked into a section of a certain library. But his recognition of ability was equally quick and clear.

There was something inspirational about Dr. Jameson. You did your very best for him at all times and never counted the effort. And he on his part never presumed on your willingness. His barbed criticism of an error was shattering. His knowledge of Colonial Office records, even though his was not firsthand knowledge, never ceased to astound. Once I remember his asking for a document which after a cursory examination I reported nonexistent. Shortly after this there came from him a postal card on which

he had written in his spidery hand the one word, "Curious."
I found the document for, of course, it was there.

In spite of his shyness, Dr. Jameson was not an absolute
conformist. For often he stepped out of this role to do the
unexpected thing.

There was the time I was vacationing with a British
friend in Portland, Maine. Dr. Jameson, who usually spent
his vacations in the same vicinity, came over one day from
his cottage in North Edgecomb to show us the glories of
Portland. We were nearing the end of our tour with only
the Longfellow museum still to be seen. This turned the conversation to Longfellow and Dr. Jameson to reciting his
"Ship of State." He was not finished when we came to a
street crossing. Undisturbed by the passersby and even
unmindful of them, he stopped on the corner and we stood
still until he had finished the poem. Then as if there had
been no interruption in our walk we went on to the museum.

With scholarship his chief interest, the effect of World
War I deeply concerned Dr. Jameson. It was not all tragic
though. The State Department was disturbed by the large
number of foreign journals and periodicals which were
sent to him. It was even then fearful of subversive activities.
The result of this, so Dr. Jameson told me, was that the
State Department sent one of its younger men to ask for
an explanation of this literature. He got it. For in a few
well chosen words, Dr. Jameson gave the bewildered young
man a free lecture on the universal scope of history and the
importance of scholarship.

I remember once telling Dr. Jameson of my interest in
politics and how little American gossipy news was available
in London at that time. And perhaps after several years in
England I may have been a little homesick. How he managed it no one will ever know, for he did more than an
ordinary man's work every day. But thereafter until illness
made it impossible, at regular intervals in his own spidery
handwriting he sent me an account of his reactions to the
American political scene. His was a liberal outlook, his

observation succinct and penetrating. These rare letters
were destroyed when Hitler bombed London; people were
not the only war casualty.

My own interest in history, since English and Latin were
and have been my own particular loves, was brought about
by the practical reason that I was then earning my living
by it. Since I was already in Europe, to Dr. Jameson it
seemed the natural thing for me to go to the International
Congress of History which was to be held in Brussels. Induced by his urging I went, rather reluctantly I must admit.
My French at that time could only be classed as a liability.
To add to the interest of the Congress for me, Dr. Jameson
sent me two letters of introduction, one to Professor Pirenne,
the great Belgian historian and the President of the Congress,
and one to the Bollandists Society. Professor Pirenne had
been a recent guest in the home of Dr. Jameson in Washington and the Bollandists had dedicated their publication,
"The Work of the Bollandists through three centuries, 1615-
1915," to Dr. Jameson. This was done to thank him for
his untiring efforts to secure funds to enable them to continue their scholarly work which the war had grievously
interrupted.

I seldom, if ever, use letters of introduction for I have
never felt I had the right to impose on other people's time
just to indulge in polite conversation. So naturally I had
done nothing with these letters. In the meantime, Dr. Jameson had written to both Dr. Pirenne and the Bollandists
that I should be attending the Congress, and even knowing
how busy they were said that he would greatly appreciate
their doing whatever they could for me. In both cases I was
later called upon and offered specially supervised visits to
libraries and inspection of Brussel's historical treasures.
It has been one of my great regrets that I was then too
young and ignorant in the field of history to appreciate
this rare opportunity.

Dr. Jameson's particular project of which I had personal
knowledge was the *Guides* to documents in foreign archives

relating to American history. At the time these *Guides* were compiled there were not many courses in American history given in any of our colleges or universities. And there was little opportunity to do any research in the subject since most of the necessary documents for such study were in foreign archives. For it was there the account of the beginnings of our history was to be found. The American students who then were financially able to spend the time abroad for such research were distressingly few. This was long before the time of grants from our numerous foundations and government scholarships. That these *Guides* are now mostly out of print and seldom referred to in no way detracts from the impact they made in the field of American history, nor the wide use students then made of them.

When the Carnegie Institution set an age limit on its employees, Dr. Jameson, who had expected to work as long as he was able, found that in a few years he must retire. In his view compounding the injury, the Institution decided to concentrate its funds and research facilities in archeological discoveries in Central America and thus bring the historical department to a close. This was a heavy blow to Dr. Jameson and his future plan, a graduate school for historians. On two separate occasions he told me about this in great detail. This was not due to forgetfulness but rather marked the depth of his hurt.

Dr. Jameson's achievements were formidable. But his achievements were the least remarkable feature of his career. Here was a man gifted as few men are. His learning was phenomenal, his memory awesome, he was at home in four languages, he was blessed with great wit, and he knew how to write. This he did so beautifully and clearly that there was never any mistaking his meaning.

With all these advantages he could have written great books. But he did not. Why? The reason why is the measure of his greatness. He wanted only to interest young American historians in the history of their own country and to provide them with the means to present its story fully and factually.

Such were his reasons for devoting his energies to the publication of the *Guides,* to working for a building where those records could be safely kept, to assisting in forming an American historical association, to editing a magazine equal in standard from its inception to the best of European similar publications, to giving practical aid to enable the Bollandists to continue their scholarly work when it was interrupted by war, and those other numerous activities—and they were numerous—to which he devoted his life. There was little, if any, personal gain to be had from this, entailing as it did constant committee meetings, conferences, colossal correspondence, often more tiresome than not. Necessary as these duties were, they carried no material or pecuniary gain. Yet none was neglected and the time for them was given not grudgingly but generously. This was the kind of man he was. And never did Dr. Jameson construe these acts as condescending favors. Humility and selflessness of such quality are characteristic attributes of only the very great. And surely, Dr. Jameson was one of these.

JAMESON AND AMERICAN
RELIGIOUS HISTORY

by John Tracy Ellis*

Over a decade ago in an essay entitled "How To Understand Our Past," Christopher Dawson lamented the tendency to treat secular and ecclesiastical history as self-con-
tained units. No serious historian, he said, could be satisfied
with this state of affairs since "it destroyed the intelligible
unity of culture and left the history of culture itself suspended uneasily between political and ecclesiastical history
with no firm basis in either of them."[1] While the work of
too many historians still shows this defect, it was never a
characteristic of the writing of J. Franklin Jameson. He
may, indeed, have acquired his deep respect for religious
history very early in life, for one who knew him intimately
has described the infancy and boyhood years of the future
historian as those of "a school master's son in a devout
Christian family."[2] In any case, the interest endured
throughout Jameson's long life and manifested itself in a
great variety of ways, such as the emphasis he gave to
religion in his lectures at the University of Chicago after
his transfer there in 1901, and the role he played as a
causa agitans for William H. Allison's *Inventory of Unpublished Materials for American Religious History in Protestant Church Archives and Other Repositories,* which was
published in 1910.

Those who have the best title to speak of the contributions made by Dr. Jameson would seem to be agreed that

9

among his most enduring benefactions to the historical
profession, both here and abroad, was the encouragement
so generously and patiently bestowed on all varieties of
workers in history by his constructive criticisms, his mean-
ingful suggestions, and often his kindly personal presence.
For example, while yet a young man teaching at Brown
University, he supplied a much needed stimulus to the pur-
suers of that frequently solitary and thankless task, the
cultivation of local history which, needless to say, often
has a close bearing on religious history. In a paper on the
functions of state and local historical societies, read at the
annual meeting of The American Historical Association at
Cleveland in December, 1897, he wisely counseled against
undue emphasis on genealogy and urged college teachers to
concern themselves with local history, especially in the
more recent periods of the American past. He maintained
that fresh life would be infused into every society of this
kind if its members would clearly perceive that its province
lay in "American history locally exemplified." And to Jameson the real glory of a local society would be its sponsorship
of what he described as "a series of volumes of important
historical documents, original materials selected with intelli-
gence, systematically ordered, edited ably, and with finished
scholarship."[3] In fact, after reading this paper written
nearly seventy years ago the local historian—whether of
religion of the 1960's or of secular life—might well wonder
how he could improve upon it, beyond adding the uses to
which mechanical and scientific devices like microfilm, unknown when Jameson wrote, are now put.

The service that this distinguished scholar performed
for the devotees of state and local history was duplicated
for the ecclesiastical historian proper ten years later in his
choice of subject for the presidential address before The
American Historical Association at Madison in December,
1907. In a significant paper to which he gave the title, "The
American Acta Sanctorum,"[4] Jameson not only revealed
one of the chief aspects of his personal interest, but at the

outset he showed his ready acquaintance with the Middle
Ages and early modern Europe by demonstrating the in-
sight which the biographies of a nation's holy men have
at times cast on national character. Saints like Francis of
Assisi, Louis IX of France, Joan of Arc, Ignatius Loyola,
and Francis Xavier were cited as examples of what he had
in mind. Jameson stated that his principal purpose was to
call attention to an analogous body of material which was at
the command of students of American history, and which
was contained, he said, in "numberless little books, shabby
and faded, printed most often on provincial presses and
seldom straying far from the place of origin."[5] The personal
accounts of colonial missionaries like Jacques Marquette and
Junipero Serra were to Jameson cases in point where a
student was able to see the Indians of the seventeenth and
eighteenth centuries as he could nowhere else, while the
social milieu of early nineteenth-century Americans was
to be found best portrayed, he thought, in the writings of
the Methodist circuit riders.

It was Jameson's belief that through media of this kind
there was gradually unveiled what he termed "the obscure
processes of Americanization," while at the same time they
delineated something of the nation's character. As he said,
the native atmosphere of cheer and hope, as well as the
American's sense of progress, were preserved in these
sources in a way that even the rigors of ultra-Calvinism
did not wholly destroy. Therefore, the historian who wished
to understand the past and present of the United States, and
for that reason sought to provide himself with data that
would represent all classes, periods, and regions would, in
Jameson's opinion, "find in the history of American religion
the closest approach to the continuous record he desires."[6]
He remarked that in this country religious history held an
especially close relationship to a history of the people's general spirit because in the United States, more than any-
where else, the affairs of the churches (and here the
Catholic Church would have to be excepted) "have been

managed by the laity or in accordance with their will." If
in every other period of recorded time the study of religion
had cast a revealing light on the multiple aspects of man's
past why, he asked, should it be otherwise with the religious
history of the United States? The aim of all students of
American history should be to seek to know the broad story
of the nation's culture from every possible angle, and in
urging their pursuit of that goal, Jameson concluded:

> Most of all, let us seek it from the history of
> American religion, in the sum total an ample
> record, even though in parts we have to compose
> it like a mosaic from fragments of unpromising
> material.[7]

The counsel that Jameson had given in 1897 to the fol-
lowers of local history in urging them to sponsor the search-
ing out and editing of original source materials, remained
a favorite theme throughout his long professional career.
For example, less than two weeks after his Madison address
on the importance of American religious history, he followed
it up with a strong plea to Robert S. Woodward, President
of the Carnegie Institution of Washington—whose staff
Jameson had joined in 1905—for funds to help finance a
trip to Europe for Carl Russell Fish, associate professor of
American history in the University of Wisconsin, in order
that the latter might make a survey of archival depositories
for documents pertaining to the history of this country. He
was especially anxious that Fish should examine the Vatican
Archives since, as he told Woodward, ". . . it is to be borne
in mind that most of the area of the United States was
before the beginning of the nineteenth century under Catholic control, and all of it since that date has had more or
less relation with the papacy." The man who would do this
job properly would have to know Spanish and Italian, and
Fish qualified on this count. Moreover, besides a knowledge
of languages, the task called for a person who possessed
what Jameson called "unusual qualities of address, tact,
acute perception, diplomatic skill and social experience."

All these, he felt, were present in his former Brown student, as well as the ability to work well with others. True, Fish was not a Catholic, but on that point Jameson remarked:

> I may add that while there are a few places (only a few) in Rome where a Catholic might do better than a Protestant, I know of no Catholic who has enough knowledge of American history to do the task anything like as well as Professor Fish; and that he as a High Church Episcopalian will have many of the same advantages in Rome that a Catholic might have.

That there was no American Catholic in 1908 with the professional training and experience demanded by Jameson was true, although it is not immediately apparent how he thought Fish as a high church Episcopalian would be in an equally advantageous position to a Catholic at the Holy See. In any case, Jameson's own shrewd inquiries on an earlier visit to Rome had convinced him that entrance to the archives of the Holy Office and of the Congregation de Propaganda Fide—which he particularly wished to have investigated— would not be easily gained. In that connection he told Woodward:

> Access to them is to be obtained only through diplomatic skill and special favor. I went into the matter when in Rome sufficiently to perceive that such skill would be requisite in order to achieve the desired results.[8]

It was not very long, however, after the Carnegie Institution had supplied Fish with the necessary funds that the "desired results" were forthcoming in the young scholar's *Guide to the Materials for American History in Roman and Other Italian Archives* (1911), a work that for over half a century has proved highly useful to numerous students, and for which much credit was owed to Jameson.

It must have been immensely encouraging to the few and isolated workers in American religious history in 1907 to have the President of The American Historical Association lend the prestige of his office and name to so strong an affirmation of the prime importance of their specialization. Up to the time of Jameson's Madison speech the churches had done little of a significant character to promote their own history, and his presidential address may well have furnished in part the inspiration that prompted a small group of Catholic historians seven and a half years later to launch a scholarly publication in church history. It was in April, 1915, that there appeared the first issue of *The Catholic Historical Review,* a quarterly edited by members of the faculty of The Catholic University of America. Jameson's advice had been sought in advance by the editors and, writing as editor of *The American Historical Review* less than two years after the beginning of the new journal, he told William W. Rockwell, librarian and assistant professor of history in Union Theological Seminary, that he welcomed additional periodicals that would cover particular sections or aspects of the general field of history whenever he saw a prospect of their success, to which he added:

> . . . and in the field of church history where *The Catholic Historical Review* is making very creditable progress, I should be delighted to see a good journal produced by the Protestant scholars; still more so if it were produced by both Protestants and Catholics, inasmuch as *The Catholic Historical Review* seems to intend to confine itself to the history of Catholicism in America.[9]

He encouraged Rockwell to aim at a new journal for which, he thought, one of the more affluent Protestant seminaries might be induced to put up the money. In his opinion both the Catholics and the Jews had done "a great deal more for *American* church history in the last thirty years than any, if not all, of the Protestant denominations," and he felt that the time had now come to tap Protestant resources for a like purpose.[10]

Not only had Jameson been helpful in getting *The Catholic Historical Review* underway, but he and his close associate and friend, Waldo G. Leland—who like Jameson was not of the Catholic faith—also gave conspicuous aid to one of the *Review's* editors, Father Peter Guilday, when the latter began to plan for a national society devoted to the history of the Catholic Church. Early in 1917 Leland contributed an article to *The Catholic Historical Review* which he called "Concerning Catholic Historical Societies."[11] He, too, was of the opinion that the American Catholics had done "much more for their history than have any of the Protestant denominations."[12] Dr. Leland saw the Catholic Church as admirably suited to organize historical activities by reason of its administrative divisions into dioceses which could foster the development of archives, museums, and libraries on the diocesan level and thus contribute toward building up the basic structure of a national society. He felt a national society would have a beneficial influence on the historical instruction provided in Catholic schools, and he thought another profitable goal might well be the creation of an American institution at Rome which could act as a center for the exploration of the contents of ecclesiastical archives, for the copying throughout Europe of documents relating to American Catholicism, and for the sponsorship of a publication to which he would give the name, *Monumenta Ecclesiastica Statuum Foederatorum.*

It was an ambitious program, to be sure, but his friend Jameson would undoubtedly have seconded it. Unfortunately, neither the institute at Rome nor the *Monumenta* was ever realized, but the national society for Catholic history was born less than three years later. And at its birth Jameson stood, so to speak, as sponsor and helped to nurse the infant through its first days until it had gained strength and support sufficient to make it a viable body. It was in Cleveland on December 30, 1919, that a group of about fifty Catholic historians responded to the call of Dr. Guilday, who at that time was an instructor in church history in The Catholic University of America, for founding The American Catholic Historical Association. The next year at Washington the new society held its first annual meeting when its membership roster stood at 155 with fifty-seven

life members and ninety-eight annual members. At this
time it became known how highly Jameson, then Director
of the Division of Historical Research of the Carnegie Institution of Washington, was regarded by the professional
historians of the Catholic Church. The fact is best conveyed
in the remarks made on the occasion by Guilday when he
said:

> We are honored this morning by the presence
> of one who was present in Saratoga as a Founder
> of the Association [The American Historical As-
> sociation was founded there in 1884]. Doctor
> Jameson may not be known personally to the ma-
> jority of those present at this meeting, but those
> of us who have enjoyed his friendship have
> learned to esteem him as a sincere admirer of the
> historic past of our Church, as one whose life has
> been given generously and uncomplainingly to
> the steady advance of historical study in this
> country and abroad. We are fortunate in having
> him among us this morning, thirty-five years
> afterwards, at the inaugural session of this new
> national Catholic Historical Association, and I
> rejoice to have the opportunity at this auspicious
> moment to pay to him a tribute of high regard
> and appreciation for all he has done during the
> past generation in making Catholic history better
> understood.[13]

The wise counsel of Dr. Jameson was at the disposal of
the founders of The American Catholic Historical Association, as it was of anyone who sincerely sought to further
historical truth. And the service he rendered the new organization was manifested when he was made an honorary
life member, a distinction that has not since been duplicated
in the more than forty years of the Association's life.
Jameson had volunteered to become a paying member at
the very outset, and he encouraged other non-Catholics to
do the same. Writing to his friend, Francis A. Christie,
less than three months after the Catholics had organized,
he stated that he was sure they would welcome Protestants,
and he remarked:

> I told the secretary, as I went out of the meeting
> in Cleveland, that I wished to be a member, and
> he was so pleased that I perceived I should have
> said so, with much emphasis, at the end of my
> remarks. (Theodore) Roosevelt would not have
> failed to do this . . .[14]

Besides the assistance rendered to new professional
journals like the *New England Quarterly*, the *Mississippi
Valley Historical Review*, the *Hispanic-American Historical
Review*, *Modern History*, and *The Catholic Historical Review*,[15] and to infant historical societies both national and
local, Jameson's dedication to the varied and multiple demands of Clio was a part of his daily living. Always alert
to anything that related to ecclesiastical history, he familiar-
ized himself with the historic sites and buildings throughout
the United States where religion had left an imprint. Thus
while in Santa Fe in the summer of 1915 he visited the old
Church of San Miguel that dated from the 1620's as well
as the Cathedral of St. Francis of Assisi, while at the same
time availing himself of an opportunity for a meeting with
John B. Pitaval, fifth Archbishop of Santa Fe, during which
they "talked archives."[16] A year later, having been to Harvard, he showed the breadth of his interest and knowledge
in ecclesiastical history—as well as his quiet sense of humor
—when he informed Leland:

> That the Harvard College Library does not
> possess the third volume of Conrad Eübel
> *Hierarchia Catholica* is a scandal of the first
> magnitude. Haskins and the others may have
> extenuating circumstances to allege, and there-
> fore I shall keep the deficiency out of the Boston
> newspapers as long as I possibly can.[17]

In the same vein Dr. Jameson never lost a chance to
assist foreign scholars whose efforts he recognized as pro-
ductive of good for ecclesiastical history. Thus in October,
1919, he issued an extended appeal to all persons interested
in historical studies to assist the famous Belgian Jesuit
scholars, the Bollandists, to resume publication of their

Analecta Bollandiana, which along with most scholarly
enterprises had been brought to a stop by the German occupation of Belgium during World War I. In gratitude for
his help, Father Hipployte Delehaye, S.J., one of the Bollandists' most renowned members, expressed their thanks to
Jameson by dedicating his volume, *A travers trois siècles.
L'oeuvre des Bollandistes, 1615-1915* (Brussels, 1920), to
the American historian, a work that was translated into
English by Frank L. Critchlow and published in 1922 by
the Princeton University Press.

Strategically situated in Washington for over thirty years
as Director of the Division of Historical Research of the
Carnegie Institution (1905-1927), as Managing Editor of
The American Historical Review (1905-1928), and as Chief
of the Division of Manuscripts of the Library of Congress
(1928-1937), it was small wonder that Jameson should
have been besieged by calls for help of one kind or another
from younger and less experienced workers in the field.
All the more was this the case because it was generally
known that he never turned a deaf ear to a sincere inquirer,
nor did he ever seem to lose patience with the constant demands of outsiders on his time and talent. One of his co-
workers remarked in that connection:

> The kindness, the courtesy, and the sense of the
> obligation of his position which dictated this
> policy were essential characteristics of Jameson.
> Yet it is undoubtedly true that letters, frequently
> trivial, were answered with an expenditure of
> time which might well have been applied to more
> valuable services or even to relaxation and re-
> freshment of spirit.[18]

All the while his special interest in religious history kept
him on the *qui vive* for new and original articles, as well as
for books whether in print or in manuscript. For example,
in March, 1919, Martha L. Edwards, then of Lake Erie
College and later an assistant professor of history in the
University of Wisconsin, published a significant article
called "Religious Forces in the United States, 1815-1830,"

in *The Mississippi Valley Historical Review*. Jameson wrote
her a long and enthusiastic letter in which he stated how
impressed he had been by the record of "the war work of
various denominations in Ohio," and it prompted him to
say that in his opinion actions of that kind had contributed
much more to unify American Christians than, as he said,
"all the efforts the various denominations and ecclesiastics
have made toward 'Church unity.'" He reminisced about
the differences between the churches in his home town in
New England when he was a boy, remarking how little
progress the ecumenical movement had made among them
save through the co-operation they shared in good works
that were common to them all.

Miss Edwards' article had likewise recalled to Jameson
a statement made to him some years before by the famous
Russian religious leader, Professor Paul Miliukov, to the
effect that in spite of the entire freedom enjoyed by Americans in religious matters, they had produced little of an
original character in the churches to which they gave their
spiritual allegiance. They still adhered almost entirely to
denominations of European origin, which caused Jameson
to remark, "Freedom of religious thought has in the main
not caused Americans to think freely on religious subjects."
To his mind, Billy Sunday's appeals were based on no other
thoughts respecting the Bible or theology than those which
were current in 1850, and admittedly Sunday reached and
influenced more of the average run of Americans than most
religious leaders. Jameson cited Bryan's *The Prince of
Peace*[19] as the most popular of all religious discourses in
the United States; yet he had been told its theology was
that of sixty years before. And John Alexander Dowie, to
whom he had himself listened while he held spellbound an
audience of 5,000 or more, had no other ideas than those of
what Jameson described as "the lower-middle-class British
evangelist of the fifties." As far as Jameson could see, all
the work in biblical criticism of the previous half century
had left most Americans absolutely unaffected, even though

everyone read newspapers and at least a little bit of modern
biblical criticism filtered into the pages every month or so.

Dr. Jameson was looking forward to the work that Miss
Edwards had projected on the American Indians. And that
reminded him of another digression, namely, how the Indians' story revealed "a strange evidence of human stupidity
and narrow-mindedness." Hardly any of the thousands of
good Protestants who devoted themselves to the history of
the Christian missions paid the slightest attention to what
Jameson called "the wonderful achievements in that line
of the Catholic church, or are willing to rate them as of
any serious consequence." He had seen, for example, a 400-
page book on the history of the Christian missions that
did not devote so much as two pages to Catholic efforts,
although for nearly two centuries after the birth of Protes-
tantism, its history, with slight exceptions, was devoid of
the missionary spirit. In fact, up to around 1730 Christian
mission history was almost entirely a Catholic enterprise,
and Jameson believed one could still shock 999 out of a
thousand Protestant Sunday school teachers with the additional statement that during the two centuries since 1730
the Catholic Church has been the world's chief organization
for the promotion of Christianity.[20]

The same concern on Jameson's part for proper acknowl-
edgment of the services of Catholics showed itself four
years later. He had read in manuscript several chapters of
the book of Henry K. Rowe, a former student, who was then
professor of history in Andover-Newton Theological School,
a work, incidentally, that was published in 1924 as *The History of Religion in the United States.* Jameson confessed
that Rowe might be expected to have the Baptists and
Congregationalists chiefly in mind, but he felt he had
neglected the Catholics which, he said, was "a very usual
omission among Protestant writers on the history of religious work in America." He had seen books from which
a reader would gather that nothing serious was owed to
Catholic missionaries for the evangelization of the western

world, whereas for nearly two centuries after the Reformation practically all missionary activity was in Catholic hands because the other churches were too exclusively national in their organization and outlook to devote much time or energy to the foreign missions. And in colonial America, the efforts of John Eliot and the Mayhews, which were about all that American Puritanism had to show, were to Jameson "hardly a drop in the bucket compared to what the Catholics were doing at that time." He presumed that Rowe was familiar with Catholic mission literature as it was found in the first six volumes of *The Catholic Historical Review,* although, he added, "such knowledge does not show out adequately in your narrative."

In conclusion Jameson advised Rowe that if he was going to say anything about the Catholic missions, his point concerning the "necessary deflection of the missionary activities from frontier regions to cities" had special pertinence for the Catholics. Until the Civil War, he explained, the Catholic missionaries' principal occupation was reaching, gathering together, and confirming the wandering sheep who had become more or less isolated in the rural areas. But the tremendous Catholic immigration of the previous thirty years —particularly that of the Italians and the Slavs—had gone to the cities and had become part of the industrial rather than the agricultural society of this country. There was a difference, therefore, in the direction of the American Catholics' home missions as well as differences of nationality and language. This truth was driven home, Jameson remarked, when one saw a Polish inscription on a fine new Catholic church in Northampton, Massachusetts, or found a multitude of Slavic names in a list of Catholic clergy in the ecclesiastical Provinces of St. Paul, Milwaukee, and Chicago.[21]

If the main emphasis here has been on Jameson's relationship to Catholic historical affairs, rather than those of Protestant and Jewish connection, it is due in part to the fact that this aspect of the religious history of the United

States appears more frequently in his printed correspondence, as well as to the writer's greater familiarity with the
story of Catholic life in the United States. That Jameson
did not contribute very much personally to the printed
literature on American religious history is evident from the
fact that one finds only three references to his name in the
two-volume work of Nelson R. Burr *et al., A Critical Bibliography of Religion in America* (Princeton, 1961). And of
those three references, two are to his presidential address
of 1907 and the third to the religious items to be found in
his *Dictionary of United States History* (Philadelphia,
1931).

The principal contribution of J. Franklin Jameson to
American religious history consisted, then, in the encouragement he gave to others, and his generous sharing of the
rich knowledge he had of American history and its sources
which enabled him to offer so much intelligent and meaning-
ful direction to younger and less experienced workers. Yet
Jameson never took himself so seriously as to frighten off
others. For example, after his detailed reactions to Miss
Edwards' article of March, 1919, he concluded on a light
note by saying: "But anybody would think I was still a
professor, and still lecturing. I congratulate you upon the
good field you have, and the good work you are doing in
it."[22] The constant harassment from the ceaseless calls for
his help never caused him to lose his tranquility of spirit.
Thus probably not many men whose days were as crowded
with important assignments and tasks as those of Jameson
would conclude a long letter of advice to a former student on
a manuscript sent for his critical judgment by saying:
"I return your chapters. Thank you very much for the
opportunity to read them."[23] This was courtesy that went
beyond the call of duty, but it insured to Jameson not only
a more enduring name in the professional circles through
which he moved with so much ease and personal enjoyment
for over forty years, but, too, of a lasting place in the hearts
of hundreds who, beyond being enlightened by his wise and

learned counsel, were charmed by the great scholar's gracious and courtly manner.

NOTES

* Monsignor Ellis is professor of church history in the University of San Francisco.

1 Christopher Dawson, *Understanding Europe* (New York, 1952), p. 13.

2 Waldo G. Leland, "John Franklin Jameson," *Dictionary of American Biography, Supplement Two*, XXII, p. 339.

3 "The Functions of State and Local Historical Societies with Respect to Research and Publication," *Annual Report of the American Historical Association for the Year 1897* (Washington, 1898), p. 59.

4 *American Historical Review*, XIII (January, 1908), Pp. 286-302.

5 *Ibid.*, p. 291.

6 *Ibid.*, p. 298.

7 *Ibid.*, p. 302.

8 Jameson to Woodward, January 8, 1908, Elizabeth Donnan and Leo F. Stock (Eds.), *An Historian's World, Selections from the Correspondence of John Franklin Jameson* (Philadelphia, 1956), Pp. 115-16. Hereafter this work will be referred to as Donnan-Stock.

9 Jameson to Rockwell, January 29, 1917, *ibid.*, p. 205.

10 *Ibid.*

11 *Catholic Historical Review*, II (January, 1917), Pp. 386-99.

12 *Ibid.*, p. 390.

13 "The American Catholic Historical Association," *Catholic Historical Review*, VI (April, 1920), p. 6.

14 Jameson to Christie, March 12, 1920, Donnan-Stock, p. 249.

15 *Ibid.*, p. 10.

16 Jameson to Leland, Santa Fe, June 25, 1915, *ibid.*, p. 180.

17 Jameson to Leland, North Edgecomb, Maine, July 21, 1916, *ibid.*, p. 199. Charles Homer Haskins was Harvard's outstanding medievalist at the time; Volume III of Eübel's work had appeared in 1910.

18 Donnan-Stock, p. 8.

19 This was the title of William Jennings Bryan's favorite public lecture (Chicago, 1909), which he gave numerous times over a long period of years.

20 Jameson to Edwards, November 19, 1919, *ibid.*, Pp. 247-48.

21 Jameson to Rowe, December 18, 1923, *ibid.*, p. 295.

22 *Ibid.*, p. 248.

23 *Ibid.*, p. 295.

JAMESON AND THE LIST OF DOCTORAL DISSERTATIONS IN HISTORY

by William Lloyd Fox

J. Franklin Jameson established the publication of the *List of Doctoral Dissertations in History in Progress or Completed at Colleges and Universities in the United States since 19—* as one of his many contributions to the field of historical scholarship. With his customary foresight he saw the advantage of a "clearing house" of such information for student and professor alike.

It was in February, 1897, while he was teaching at Brown University that Jameson circulated a typewritten list of the names of thirty-four doctoral candidates and the titles of their dissertations. The institutions represented on that first list of doctoral dissertations in history, which bore the title "Candidates for the Doctor's Degree in American History and Their Theses," included Brown, Bryn Mawr, Columbia, Cornell, Harvard, Johns Hopkins, Michigan, Pennsylvania, Radcliffe, and Wisconsin. Of the three candidates from Wisconsin whose names appeared on Jameson's original list, two were to become presidents of The American Historical Association: Carl L. Becker (1931) and Herbert E. Bolton (1932).

Jameson was quite aware that the distribution of a list of dissertation titles "... does not wholly prevent men from taking subjects which are already in a sense preempted; but," as he dryly added, "it is a free country." The publica-

tion of the titles, however, tended to lessen the duplication
and serious overlapping of dissertation subjects.

Not long after the establishment of the *List of Doctoral
Dissertations in History in Progress,* Jameson expanded it
to include all historical topics, not just those dealing with
the American past. Beginning in 1902, he had the *List*
printed. In the meantime he had been appointed chairman
of the history department of the University of Chicago,
a position he was to occupy until 1905. Thirteen years after
he established the *List* Jameson received an offer from Dr.
Albert E. McKinley to have it printed in *The History
Teacher's Magazine.* Having always paid for the *Lists* out
of his own pocket, Jameson gladly accepted McKinley's
offer. In *The History Teacher's Magazine* for January, 1913,
the list of doctoral dissertation titles for 1912 was published;
but during the next four years the *Lists* were printed in the
January numbers of *The American Historical Review.* Between 1918 and 1939 they were published by the Department
of Historical Research of the Carnegie Institution of Washington, the department which Jameson served as director
from 1905 until 1928 when he became Chief of the Division
of Manuscripts, Library of Congress. The American Historical Association commenced to publish in 1939 an annual
List of Doctoral Dissertations in History, although publication was suspended from 1941 to 1947. Since 1947, seven
Lists have been compiled, the last one (1964) having included the names and the titles of dissertations of more than
two thousand registrants, an impressive contrast with the
number comprising the first *List.*

Besides serving as a means for avoiding the duplication
of effort in the preparation of dissertations, the *List* has
provided a valuable index of changing interest and emphasis
in historical studies. Thus one can see from a perusal of
recent *Lists* a growing interest in such fields as American
social and intellectual history and the history of the Far
East.

After editing the *List of Doctoral Dissertations in His-*

tory for many years, Jameson came to believe that some of
the topics selected for theses were unfortunate and ill-
suited to the needs and experience of graduate students.
He thought that there was a rather disturbing trend towards
the lengthening of doctoral dissertations in history. Writing
in December, 1926, to Professor Marcus W. Jernegan, who
was preparing a report on the "Productivity of Doctors of
Philosophy in History" (*The American Historical Review*,
October, 1927), Jameson observed (Elizabeth Donnan and
Leo F. Stock, eds., *An Historian's World: Selections from
the Correspondence of John Franklin Jameson* [Philadel-
phia: American Philosophical Society, 1956, p. 322]) :

> It seems possible if a young man began with a
> small publication, treating a very limited subject,
> that he would feel more encouraged to go on later
> to produce something large in that field or in
> some other field.
>
> Forty years ago, as I can well remember, doc-
> toral dissertations were not so formidable. They
> were of about the size current in German univer-
> sities. Now, we have advanced to the size of the
> French or Russian theses, but we have not done
> so because we have removed the doctorate to a
> higher grade of advancement, some ten years
> after the baccalaureate, as in the French or Rus-
> sian case, but, I fear, because the unhallowed
> competitive ambitions of universities have drawn
> them into a desire to produce bigger disserta-
> tions than their competitors—"the world's big-
> gest theses."

With his establishment of the *List of Doctoral Dissertations in History* as a small but important publication, with
his superior editing of *The American Historical Review*,
with his distinguished service in the Carnegie Institution
of Washington, in the Library of Congress, and on the Historical Manuscripts Commission, Jameson did what he
came to believe was his true function in the American historical profession: To make bricks, as he modestly put it,
for others to use. For the building materials which he strove
to provide, American historians are forever in his debt.

J. FRANKLIN JAMESON AND THE ORIGIN OF THE NATIONAL HISTORICAL PUBLICATIONS COMMISSION*

by Waldo Gifford Leland

As you enter the National Archives Building from Pennsylvania Avenue you may see, at the left of the lobby, a bronze portrait plaque placed there in December, 1955, by The American Historical Association "IN TRIBUTE TO J. FRANKLIN JAMESON 1859-1937 WHOSE PERSISTENT AND WISE GUIDANCE LED TO THE ESTABLISHMENT OF THE NATIONAL ARCHIVES."

Although Jameson lived to see the monumental success of his long campaign for the National Archives, he witnessed only the nominal success of his much longer and more difficult campaign for a National Historical Publications Commission. It remained for others, especially for Dr. Philip Hamer, first Executive Director of the Commission and his successor, Dr. Oliver W. Holmes, to bring to full fruition Jameson's hopes and plans. The tradition of Jameson's scholarship and of his great services to American historical studies is still lively although there are now very few who were his students, colleagues or associates, and it may be useful to many readers of this paper to have a brief summary of his career. He was born in September 1859, the son of a Boston schoolmaster, John Jameson, and on his mother's side a lineal descendant of Capt. Edward Johnson, first historian of New England and author of *The Wonder-Working Providence of Sion's Saviour in New England.* Jameson was graduated from Amherst College in 1879, standing first in his class. At commencement he delivered an oration bearing the simple title of "Buddha."

From his first year at Amherst he resolved to devote his lifework to the study and teaching of history, for which indeed he had unusual qualifications in the form of a remarkable memory, an orderly mind in which he could store information with the power of instant recall, and a constructive imagination. After graduation and a year of high school teaching, being unable to find funds for an ambitious program of study in German universities, he entered the recently founded Johns Hopkins University, where he spent eight formative years as fellow and teaching associate. In 1882, he received the first doctorate in history conferred by the Hopkins and decided that American history should be his chief field of work. He made an ambitious plan for a "magnum opus" on the constitutional and political history of the States of the Union but did not go beyond publishing an "Introduction" to that formidable undertaking. More significant, in view of his future work in the laying of sound foundations for research and writing, were the copying, editing, and publication of the records (1735-88) of the Town of Amherst, and the comment in his diary, June 11, 1883: ". . . it is one of those things that every town ought to have done for it; if all did it would make an invaluable body of material for historical works of several kinds." Of similar significance during his later years at the Hopkins was his unsuccessful effort to secure permission to edit and publish the records of the Virginia Company in the possession of the Library of Congress.

Most of Jameson's writings while at the Hopkins were relevant to his master interest in solid foundations for work in American history, the filling in of gaps, and the suggestion of fresh points of view. Among such were his lectures on the history of historical writing in America (published

as a book in 1891), and his course for graduates on historical method and criticism. After the Hopkins there followed
thirteen years at Brown University (1888-1901) and four
at the University of Chicago (1901-5). These teaching years
were in turn followed by thirty-two years of administration
—twenty-three as Director of the Department of Historical
Research in the Carnegie Institution of Washington and
nine as Chief of the Division of Manuscripts in the Library
of Congress and holder of its endowed Chair of American
History. During all these years he was one of the leading
members of The American Historical Association, which
he had helped to found in 1884 and of which he became president in 1907; and from its founding in 1895 until 1928, he
was managing editor of *The American Historical Review*,
except for his four years at Chicago. He died in 1937, a
few days after his 78th birthday.

Since this paper is chiefly about Jameson's campaign
for the National Historical Publications Commission, we
must go back to the Hopkins, where he probably had his
first idea of such a body. Mention has been made of his
efforts to secure permission to edit and publish the records
of the Virginia Company in the Library of Congress. As
early as 1886, he made urgent representations not only to
the Librarian of Congress, Ainsworth Spofford, but also
to the Joint Committee on the Library of the House and
Senate, without results. Whether or not as a consequence
of Jameson's importunate demands, the Civil Appropriations Act of March 3, 1887, provided:

> that the Secretary of State, the Librarian of
> Congress, and the Secretary of the Smithsonian
> Institution, and their successors in office, are
> hereby constituted a commission whose duty it
> shall be to report to Congress, the character
> and value of the historical and other manuscripts
> belonging to the Government of the United
> States, and what method and policy should be
> pursued in regard to editing and publishing the
> same, or any of them.[1]

This sounds like a National Historical Publications Commission, at least in embryo, but no evidence has been found, in spite of diligent research, that the Commission ever held a meeting or ever reported to Congress. Jameson wrote to his father that he thought the creation of the Commission would only make it more difficult for him to secure permission to edit the papers of the Virginia Company.

The first public statement on behalf of such a commission as we now have was made by Jameson before The American Historical Association in December, 1890, in the form of a report on "The Expenditures of Foreign Governments in Behalf of History."[2] Jameson pointed out that, aside from large appropriations for compiling and publishing the *Official Records of the War of the Rebellion,* very little was expended for the publication of other records or papers of great value for many aspects of American history. He contrasted this lack of system with the careful planning in many other countries, on which he reported in detail. In conclusion he presented his proposal:

> We desire a comprehensive and well arranged scheme of government publication. We should perceive that we can not have it save by means of some permanent institution through which expert opinion can be brought to bear, not simply at the beginning, or by occasional advice, but all the time. A commission consisting simply of government officials can never meet the requirements, and this has already been shown by the result of the abortive act of March 3, 1887.
>
> . . . A suitable mode of making up and empowering a good working commission would not be difficult to devise. When the Government is ready to do this, European experience should be much consulted. In any case, such a commission should have power to edit and publish not only materials in the possession of the Government, but also those which are in private hands. May it soon come into existence.

"Soon" proved to be forty-four years, during which

Jameson was active in many ways to produce tangible results, even without a governmental commission. The American Historical Association, founded in 1884, had been incorporated by Congress on January 4, 1889, for "the collection and preservation of historical manuscripts, and for kindred purposes in the interest of American history and of history in America."[3] The association, Jameson felt, had not only the duty to accomplish the prescribed purposes but it also had a Government-recognized status. Following Jameson's proposal, the association created in 1895 a Historical Manuscripts Commission, the chief task of which should be to edit and publish in the association's annual reports, which were printed as public documents, important bodies of manuscript material relating to American history. This commission may be thought of, in some respects, as the prototype of the present Commission, and its membership deserves to be commemorated: Douglas Brymner, of Ottawa; Talcott Williams, of Philadelphia; William F. Trent, of Sewanee, Tennessee; Frederick Jackson Turner, of Madison, Wisconsin; and Jameson, of Brown University, chairman. The association's annual reports were soon swollen with edited collections of historical manuscript materials of great variety and value. Such were the correspondence of John C. Calhoun, edited by Jameson, the diplomatic archives of the Republic of Texas, dispatches from the French ministers to the United States, and many more. But Jameson found still other avenues of publication. As managing editor of *The American Historical Review* from its foundation in 1895, he set aside in each issue space for a section of documents. In the aggregate a great deal of material, both American and foreign, was made public in this manner. Jameson also appealed to the state and local historical societies of the country to publish documentary material and encouraged them to cooperate in exploring the sources of their history, whether located in Washington, as in the case of former Territories, or in foreign countries, as in the case of areas that had been under French or Spanish domination.

Towards the turn of the century historians were becoming increasingly conscious of the importance of establishing in the National Capital an active center for the advancement of historical research and publication and, in 1901, the council of The American Historical Association appointed a committee of three—Charles Francis Adams, Andrew C. McLaughlin, and Jameson, chairman—to consider the possibility of establishing in Washington a national institute for advanced historical studies. In the next year the Carnegie Institution of Washington was founded and Daniel C. Gilman, former president of The Johns Hopkins University, was appointed its first president. Jameson, who had kept Gilman informed respecting the plan for an institute of historical studies, suggested that the new institution might be interested in promoting work in that field. Gilman, who was then naming a number of advisory committees in different fields of knowledge, adopted the committee of the association as one of the institution's advisory committees and asked it to propose a plan for the organization of historical work by the institution. Such a plan was drawn up and presented in the form of a report with recommendations to the trustees of the institution. This report was printed in the first yearbook of the Carnegie Institution, along with reports by other advisory committees. The essence of the plan was the preparation and publication of guides to the sources of American history in the archives of the Federal Government and in the archives and libraries of foreign countries, and the editing and publication of collections of important documents and papers still in manuscript. Provision for editing *The American Historical Review* was also recommended.

The trustees of the Carnegie Institution adopted the recommendations of the report and proceeded to give effect to them by providing for the preparation of a guide to the archives of the Federal Government and by creating a Bureau (later Department) of Historical Research, of which McLaughlin was named organizing director. The general program was quickly underway, and when McLaughlin returned to his professorship in the University of Michigan in 1905, Jameson was appointed director of the department. Within a few months he resumed his active campaign for a National Historical Publications Commission in a paper read before the Columbia Historical Society of Washington in February, 1906, on "Gaps in the Published Records of United States History."[4] In this he presented an account of the recent creation by the Government of the Netherlands of an Advisory Committee for Historical Publications, and he rapidly reviewed the present state of historical documentary publication in the United States, strongly urging that the United States should have a commission similar in purpose and plan to that of the Netherlands. In order that such a proposal should have a vigorous sponsor Jameson turned to The American Historical Association, over which he presided in 1907, and obtained its agreement to appoint a special committee to review the needs of historical documentary publication in the United States and to propose a plan for dealing with them through a national commission. Such a committee was appointed by Jameson's successor as president of the association, George B. Adams, who named Worthington C. Ford as chairman and Jameson as secretary.

Before this committee could be organized, however, Secretary of State Elihu Root, to whom Jameson had earlier presented his plan, came forward with a suggestion on how the support of the Government might be assured—namely, by the attachment of the association's committee to the President's Committee on Department Methods, popularly known as the Keep Commission. President Theodore Roosevelt, who had approved the proposal in principle but who thought that he had no available funds for giving effect to it, agreed: and he instructed the Committee on Department Methods to adopt the committee of the association as an "assistant committee." This was promptly done and the new committee now had Government status and support. It proceeded at once to carry out its mandate and in January, 1908, presented its report, with recommended legislation, to the President, who transmitted it to the Congress a month later.[5]

Only one hearing on the bill was held—on January 5, 1910, by the House Committee on the Library. Statements in support of the bill were made by Jameson, Charles Francis Adams, Alfred T. Mahan, and Charles M. Andrews, all of whom had been members of the special committee.

The bill, which was for the creation of a Commission on National Historical Publications, never came before either House of Congress for a vote. It lay in the limbo of the files of Congress until 1934. During these years Jameson used every method and approach to bring the bill to a vote. His letters reveal how earnestly he tried to have it considered and his feeling of discouragement. In the meanwhile, however, he directed the work of the Department of Historical Research as well as his campaign for the National Archives. Under his direction the department performed many of the functions that the proposed commission might have undertaken. The department had already, in 1907, published a second and enlarged edition of the *Guide to the Archives of the Government of the United States at Washington,* and during the years it explored the archives and libraries of foreign countries, publishing some twenty volumes of guides to the materials found in them relating to American history. This operation greatly aided the project of the Library of Congress for copying such documents. The Department of Historical Research also published more than thirty large volumes of documents, which constituted major sources of the history of the United States, including *European Treaties Bearing on the History of the United States and Its Dependencies* (1917-37) ; *Letters of Members of the Continental Congress* (1912-26) ; *Proceedings and Debates of the British Parliaments Respecting North America* (1924-41) ; *Judicial Cases Concerning American Slavery and the Negro* (1926-37) ; *Documents Illustrative of the History of the Slave Trade to America* (1930-35) ; and *Correspondence of Andrew Jackson* (1926-35). Suggestions by Jameson had been responsible for numerous other publications, such as *The Records of the Federal Convention of 1787* (1911-37), edited by Max Farrand, and *Instructions*

*to the British Ministers to the United States 1791-
1812* (1941), edited by Bernard Mayo.

Jameson resolutely adhered to the original purpose of
the department, which was set forth in the 1902 report of
the advisory committee of which he had been chairman
and which he restated in 1906 in his first report as director.
The purpose was not to write historical monographs but
to make known for the benefit and use of historical scholars
the major sources of the history of the United States and
thus to lay solid foundations for their work. Of this declared
policy, he added, "for us at any rate *melius est petere fontes
quam sectari rivulos.*"

The "nominal" success of Jameson's campaign for the
National Historical Publications Commission, to which reference was made in the early paragraphs of this discourse,
came in 1934—six years after Jameson's retirement from
the Department of Historical Research and appointment
as Chief of the Division of Manuscripts in the Library of
Congress and only three years before his death. While working on the legislation governing the establishment of the
National Archives, he recognized that provision for the
National Commission could be incorporated, and this was
done. Thus set up, the Commission held three meetings, two
of which were attended by Jameson, and then lapsed into
inactivity. This was due in part to failure of the law to
provide a Secretariat for the Commission but still more to
the necessary concentration of the National Archives on its
own organization and problems. The story of the first years
of the Commission of 1934, and its failure and of its reorganization and reactivation under President Truman,
inspired by the first volume of Julian Boyd's *Papers of
Thomas Jefferson,* is well told by Dr. Hamer in his 1954
report to the Commission, which also supplements this
paper in its account of the background of the Commission.[6]

In conclusion it is fitting to name the members of the
"assistant committee" who created the National Commission on paper, though to give it life was not within their
mandate. No one of them is now living but their service

deserves to be commemorated: Worthington C. Ford, Chairman; Charles Francis Adams; Charles M. Andrews; William A. Dunning; Albert Bushnell Hart; Andrew C. McLaughlin; Alfred T. Mahan; Frederick J. Turner; J. Franklin Jameson, secretary.[7] The document signed by the above scholars should be made available to all scholars for their understanding of how a great problem was studied and for their inspiration.

NOTES

* Note: This is a second revision of a paper read by Dr. Leland before the tenth anniversary luncheon of the National Historical Publications Commission held in New York on December 29, 1960, during the annual meeting of The American Historical Association. Bearing the title "The Prehistory and Origins of the National Historical Publications Commission," it was published first in *The American Archivist* (April, 1964). It is now published in this collection, after slight further revision, with the courteous consent of the editors of the *Archivist*.

[1] 24 Stat. 542.

[2] *Annual Report of the American Historical Association for the Year 1891* (Washington, 1892), Pp. 33-61.

[3] 25 Stat. 640.

[4] Published in *The American Historical Review*, 11 (July, 1906), 817-831.

[5] 60th Cong., 2d sess., S. Doc. 714.

[6] *A National Program for the Publication of Historical Documents; a Report to the President by the National Historical Publications Commission* (Washington, 1954).

[7] The chief printed source for the work and life of J. Franklin Jameson is a collection of some 500 of his letters, from 1880 to 1937, but most abundant for the Washington period, 1905-28, edited by two former members of his staff, now deceased, Elizabeth Donnan and Leo F. Stock, with a long biographical introduction by Miss Donnan. The volume was published by the American Philosophical Society of Philadelphia in 1956, as Vol. 42 of its *Memoirs*, under the title *An Historian's World*. The Jameson papers have been presented to the Library of Congress by Francis C. Jameson of Washington, son of J. Franklin Jameson. Special attention is called to the recent masterly article by L. H. Butterfield on "Historical Editing in the United States: the Recent Past," in which several pages are devoted to Jameson as editor and as stimulator of editing (Amer. Antiq. Soc., *Proceedings*, Vol. 72, Part 2).

"INEVITABLY" THE FIRST INCUMBENT

by Verner W. Clapp

My first assignment in the Library of Congress, a temporary summer appointment, was as a cataloger in the Division of Manuscripts. This was in 1922. Dr. Charles Moore was Acting Chief of the Division, but he was concurrently Chairman of the Fine Arts Commission, and it was my impression that he delegated much of the conduct of the Division to Dr. John C. Fitzpatrick, the Assistant Chief, who had been with the Division since its creation in 1897, and who was at once its principal accessioner, arranger and cataloger, its chief of reference and its principal editor. His passion was George Washington. Under Dr. Fitzpatrick's instruction, I cataloged four collections of manuscripts that summer, including the papers of Reverdy Johnson, which, I think, Dr. Fitzpatrick gave me as an exercise in cacography.

When I returned to the Library the following year for a stay which lasted more than thirty years, it was not to the Division of Manuscripts, but to the Reading Rooms. Nevertheless, as an alumnus of the Division, able to find my way about in its collections and with many occasions for making use of them (as well as the opportunity, for my schedule gave me several free mornings a week), I took frequent advantage in the ensuing years of the unique privilege of direct access to its extraordinary resources. I was the first, I think, to go through the entire collection of

President Cleveland's papers after Professor McElroy sent
them down from Princeton; they constituted at that time,
I believe, the largest single collection in the Division and
it took months of my spare time to go through them, including the petitions, signed in their own blood, with which
the members of certain Grand Army of the Republic posts
protested to the President the return of the Confederate
flags; and I worked with many other collections as well. As
an alumnus, I was not required to work in the Pavilion
(the elaborately decorated reading room), but could use
a desk amid the manuscripts cases themselves. It was an
ideal situation.

And then in 1927, Mr. William Evarts Benjamin, the New
York book-seller, publisher and financier, endowed the Library with a Chair in American History, to be effected
through an honorarium to the chief of the Division of
Manuscripts over and above his Government stipend. It
was thus at last possible for the Librarian (Dr. Herbert
Putnam) to secure as head of the Division the outstanding
scholar for whom he had been waiting since 1917, when
Dr. Gaillard Hunt left the Division to return to the Department of State.

In consequence, Dr. Moore returned full time to the Fine
Arts Commission and Dr. Jameson was appointed to the
Chair of American History effective July 1, 1928, entering
upon duties on September 19, thereafter. At the same time
Dr. Fitzpatrick resigned to become the editor of the bicentennial *Writings of George Washington,* establishing his
headquarters almost necessarily in the Division, adjacent
to the Washington Papers. He was succeeded as Assistant
Chief by Dr. Thomas P. Martin, introduced by Dr. Putnam
as "a well-prepared archivist." At this very moment, too,
Project A (the project for enriching the resources of the
Library for studies in American history through extensive
photocopying in European libraries and archives—a project
made financially possible by Mr. John D. Rockefeller, Jr.,
but made possible in another sense only by the studies of
resources for American history which Dr. Jameson had

promoted during his long years at the Carnegie Institution) was commencing under the direction of Dr. Samuel Flagg Bemis. Dr. Jameson and Dr. Bemis met in London in the late summer of 1928, to plan the campaign for this great undertaking.

The Division, where life up to this time had been calm, now began to hum with activity. Editorial projects began to multiply: to the work on the Washington Papers and the Journals of the Continental Congress was now added the De Ricci-Wilson census of classic and medieval manuscripts, succeeded by the census of alchemic manuscripts. Photocopies resulting from Project A began to arrive in copious abundance from the national archives and principal libraries of England, France, Spain, the Netherlands, Germany, Austria, Italy, Russia and the Scandinavian countries. The staff was enlarged and strengthened by a series of eager young men, a number of whom have since found important niches in archival and manuscripts work. It was during this period, too, that the National Archives Act was approved and its building and services planned, all involving to some degree the Division of Manuscripts and its chief.

It quickly became no longer easy—or even possible—to find a vacant desk among the manuscripts cases. Also, my schedule no longer left me free of mornings. My visits to the Division became less frequent and my inquiries less extended, and these were conducted in the Pavilion rather than at the shelves. I was, however, frequently the emissary of my chief, Mr. Martin Arnold Roberts, the Superintendent of the Reading Rooms, on some business with the Division, either administration or historical fact.

So, for the near-decade in which he held the Chair of American History until the cruel accident in 1937, I was accustomed to seeing Dr. Jameson, typically not at his desk behind the curved glass screen, but standing in the Pavilion, talking in subdued tones to an inquirer, or moving quietly about the Division. His tall, slender, erect and distinguished figure left no doubt that he was the master of the house; his quietness, austerity, almost solemnity, conveyed assurance of complete dominance in that house. The urgency of my business sometimes compelled me to interrupt him; his replies on these occasions were tinged with an hauteur which seemed to say that History should not be interrupted! But always his answers were trenchant, concise, and impeccably expressed. He brought to the Library, as Dr. Putnam was to say later, "a wide, deep and extraordinarily exact knowledge of American history"; he would answer my questions precisely and completely in a single sentence, and his answers were characterized by the same felicity of expression as when he spoke of the editing of the Washington Papers as having been placed "almost inevitably" in the hands of Dr. Fitzpatrick.

Of Dr. Jameson it may be said that he was "inevitably" the first incumbent of the Chair of American History.

THE SAGE AND THE YOUNG MAN

by Allan Nevins

A high, slender, frail-looking birch tree rustling with dry leaves—this was the image that sprang to my mind as I first saw Dr. Jameson moving about his desk in the Library of Congress; so tall, stiffly erect, soberly dressed, deliberate of movement, and austere in manner as in speech. To a young man he seemed the embodiment of gravity, dignity, and scholarly conscientiousness. He was clearly a man of strong character; a gentleman of the old school, with a strong infusion of Puritan earnestness; at first sight not at all genial, but aloof and reserved. It was in 1924 that, seizing odd week-ends from my duties on the editorial staff of the *New York World* to delve in the Manuscript Division, I came to know the great scholar. I was beginning work on a life of Grover Cleveland. And as I was seeing a good deal of politics and politicians in New York and Washington, it was not strange that from my busy corner in journalism I should momentarily think him not only stiff, but a bit juiceless or desiccated.

But only momentarily! The first impression of austerity and scholarly dedication was of course deepened as our acquaintance matured into friendship. Meanwhile, all my notions of aridity and aloofness were swiftly dispelled. He rustled to my segment of the big circular reading-room desk at noon the first day and whispered, "Won't you join us for

41

lunch at the Round Table?" I comprehended that this was
not merely an accolade of which any novice in the school
of scholarly knighthood could be proud, but an expression
of special kindness. Here was the Bayard of historical at-
tainments, unsurpassed in learning, rich in experience and
honors, encouraging a wight who had yet won no spurs. No
doubt his interest in me owed something to the fact that
he had read a chapter on reform and social change in my
then recent book on the American States, 1775-1789. A little
later, to my gratification, he saw to it that his now classic
volume, *The American Revolution Considered as a Social
Movement,* was sent to me by *The American Historical Review* for a critical estimate. He knew also that I had worked
on the *Nation* when it was still a fine scholarly weekly. But
I soon perceived that kindliness was one of his integral
traits, and a readiness to give countenance to ambitious
young men was a prime element in his zeal for the invigora-
tion of historical work.

When we lunched at Herbert Putnam's Round Table, or
talked in the extra hour he sometimes allowed me after the
Manuscript Division formally closed, or walked together,
for he greatly enjoyed long walks, I found him full of dry
humor, sober anecdote, and Johnsonian remarks—that is,
wittily epigrammatic observations. He treasured up preg-
nant sayings. I remember his telling me that Mandell
Creighton, whom he knew as founder of the *English Historical Review,* had once rebuked some remark on American
crudity with the emphatic statement: "Not a bit too crude
for me! I don't cross the Atlantic to see a washed-out copy
of Europe." He had a crisp way of indicating, in measured,
judicial phrases, his disdain for some public figures of the
day: George Harvey, for example, or Henry Cabot Lodge.
But his talk never had the slightest malice, and was often
warmed by evidence of his deep affection for friends. He
once spoke with emotion of his close associate George L.
Burr of Cornell University, who for more than a decade
had helped him edit *The American Historical Review.* "I recall how Burr brought his bride to Washington in 1907,"

he said. (Burr had then just married Martha Martin of Virginia.) "I met them at the station and took them to my house. How happy they were! And in a little more than a year she was dead. He was crushed!"

On another occasion he spoke to me of his friendship with Woodrow Wilson, whom he held in affectionate admiration. The two had been fellow students at Johns Hopkins University, and kindred spirits for years afterward. "Nobody who writes on Wilson can underrate his deep religious feeling," said Jameson. "I paid a visit to Wesleyan College when he was teaching there, in 1888 or 1889. On Sunday morning I decided to go for a long walk in the Connecticut countryside. As I set off I encountered Wilson striding down the street, a Bible under his arm. 'Oh, come with me for my walk,' I said. But he waved me aside. 'Oh, no,' he replied, 'my church means far too much to me.' " The terms in which Jameson spoke of Calvin Coolidge, with whom he had a certain link in their position as Amherst alumni, were very different.

In my work on Grover Cleveland, Dr. Jameson took so cordial an interest that I suspected he might have been a Mugwump in the election of 1884, when he could have cast his second vote for President. I never asked him, for a simple reason: I thought he might regard his position in the Library as one that made expressions of party allegiance undesirable. He had far more delicacy of feeling than most men. Of his own historical work he always spoke with excessive modesty. I was an admirer of his *History of Historical Writing in America,* but he met my references to that set of lectures with deprecating words. "You know, I have never written a book," he would say. The implication of this remark was that while he was an organizer and inspirer of manifold historical activities, he had never been vouchsafed leisure for any historical composition of his own; and it was true that his inestimable services to history did not lie in the written word. Behind his modesty lay a certain shyness, and he was unquestionably happiest when working valiantly behind the scenes, with an anonymity that let other men take more credit for the result than they deserved.

Then our relationship was lighted up by a quite wonderful occurrence, as it seemed to me at the time; a remarkable illustration of his kindly interest in young men. The labors in which many had joined, with Dr. Jameson as leader, to give the country a Dictionary of American Biography comparable with the British D. N. B., were coming to fruition. The American Council of Learned Societies, the *New York Times,* and various scholars and men of affairs had pooled their energies. A Committee of Management had been appointed, with Dr. Jameson as chairman, to take the final steps. Sometime in the late summer of 1924, Dr. Jameson telephoned me at the *World* from Washington. Would I have dinner with him the next week at the Algonquin Hotel? I agreed. We enjoyed a pleasant talk while we ate; and then over the coffee cups he startled me with an unexpected proposal. Would I allow him to present my name to the Committee as editor? If I consented, he would give me his full support.

This suggestion, as astonishing as it was sudden, seemed to me unrealistic. Nobody knew better than I the reasons why a young newspaperman, who had done no postgraduate work in history, and who had no academic standing, no proved ability as a writer, and no experience in editing large-scale works, was an unlikely candidate for such a post. Nevertheless, Dr. Jameson insisted, and with many misgivings, I said I would let him propose my name.

This was something more than an illustration of Dr. Jameson's kindly interest in neophytes who in his estimation held some promise; it was a proof that his warm sympathies sometimes carried him too far. My transfer to such a post would have been a misfortune both to the Dictionary and to me, for I was interested in writing, not editing. Nobody was better pleased than I when Allen Johnson was chosen for the position. One bit of evidence that Dr. Jameson had really pressed my name with vigor lay in the fact that Johnson, to my astonishment, promptly offered me the associate editorship; an offer which I just as promptly declined. As I began to combine teaching at Columbia with continued work on the *World,* and as Dr. Jameson's health became uncertain, I saw less of him. Whenever our ways crossed, however, I endeavored to make plain not only my valuation of the debt I owed him, but my sense of the fact he was even more distinguished as a man than as a scholar—that his devotion to high standards, his tireless industry, and his gentleness made him one of the rare spirits who, in Matthew Arnold's phrase, are "sage without hardness"; who "see life steadily and see it whole."

HOPE FOR THE YOUNG SCHOLAR:
AN UNREALIZED DREAM

by Mary R. Dearing

Although J. Franklin Jameson relinquished direct contact with students when he went from the University of Chicago to Carnegie Institution, he continued throughout his life his concern for the young historical scholar, especially the graduate student. Jameson's estimate of his own potentialities as writer and teacher was unduly modest, but he did credit himself with "some, though not the best qualities," for directing graduates.[1] His continued willingness to give generously of his time to guide them by means of personal interviews as well as correspondence is well known, as is also their response to him in respect and affection. His campaign in their interests was unending; he remained ever hopeful of finding funds to aid their research. "While university organization in the United States remains what it is," he wrote to Daniel Coit Gilman, "subsidies cannot give the older men the chance for original work on a large scale. To subsidize the younger men, on the other hand, is to make it easier to write doctoral dissertations, to increase the quantity and improve the quality of the more immature part of the work now done."[2] As The American Historical Association established prizes for monographs, it was Jameson's hope that the younger men especially would strive for them.[3]

Jameson's most successful project for the fledgling scholar was, unquestionably, his periodically published *List of Doc-*

46

toral Dissertations in History. Another project to which
he devoted considerable effort over the years might have
constituted an even greater encouragement had it worked
out as he hoped: this was his dream of a research center in
Washington for graduate history students.

The stimulus for this idea seems to have been the paper
that Professor Lucy M. Salmon delivered in Washington,
December 29, 1900, at the annual meeting of The American
Historical Association. In "An American School of History
at Rome," she presented the need for an establishment in
Europe where American students could receive "sympathetic
instruction and counsel" in their research.[4] Soon after this
meeting Jameson began urging that a center for graduate
students in history be established in Washington. He gave
credit to Frederick Jackson Turner for the idea, but it was
Jameson who carried the idea forward through the years.
He visualized this center as "a cross between the American
school at Athens or Rome and the Prussian or Austrian Institute für Gesichtsforschung," in which, as he later put it,
American history students might avail themselves of the
"advantages presented by the national capital, for archival
study or for political observation, under the guidance of
qualified teachers released from the sustaining universities
in rotation, on leaves of absence."[5]

When Jameson learned of the unrestricted bequest of
Herbert B. Adams to The American Historical Association
for historical purposes, he suggested that it might be devoted to this project.[6] He also produced a printed statement
of his plan which he sent not only to members of The American Historical Association executive council, of which he
and Turner were members, but to Daniel Coit Gilman as
well. When the council appointed a committee composed of
Jameson, Andrew C. McLaughlin, and James Ford Rhodes
to consider the proposal, McLaughlin commented that it was
"in a very great degree a question of finance." When he
learned about Andrew Carnegie's contribution of ten million
dollars in the interests of research, McLaughlin was elated,

for such a fund could well "bear both Rome and Washington"; "Miss Salmon's scheme" as well as Jameson's.[7]

Jameson, too, was hopeful, but for him a more compelling general interest came first; he wanted to see as much as possible of that fund devoted to the historical field. On his suggestion the committee agreed to request that the council replace this committee with one " 'on the promotion of historical research in Washington,' i.e., a committee to wait and see what the Carnegie Institution could be persuaded to do for history." Accepting this proposal, the council reappointed the same group with the addition of the retiring American Historical Association president Charles Francis Adams, because, as Jameson commented, "he knows Mr. Carnegie well."[8]

Now Jameson wrote again to Gilman, president of the new Carnegie Institution, this time urging the general cause of history and mentioning only as one of several projects the possibility of a Washington research center.[9] After the efforts of Jameson and his committee, added to those of *The American Historical Review's* board of editors, were successful in achieving the establishment within the Carnegie Institution of a Department of Historical Research,[10] Jameson resumed his plea for a Washington center. McLaughlin, chosen to head the new department (an appointment that Jameson had rather hoped to receive[11]), was still favorably disposed to the idea. "Perhaps I have most at heart the establishment of headquarters for research students in Washington," he wrote to Jameson. "I feel quite sure that things are going to work out along the lines that you have at heart."[12] The trustees did not share McLaughlin's enthusiasm, however, and refused to provide funds for student research in Washington.[13] Later Jameson was to comment sadly, "For a time, the establishment of the Department of Historical Research . . . pushed the project into the background, but that institution from the beginning left educational work out of its programme."[14]

Jameson, however, never lost sight of his dream. It

seemed, indeed, even more important to him because of the steady increase in historical resources at the nation's capital. In 1916, he conferred at Columbia University with a group of historians, "all of whom were in favor of something being done." The committee they appointed drew up a constitution for a residential center which would offer facilities to students of political science and economics as well as history; this center would be under the control of the departments of those universities that contributed to its support. Jameson, reporting to McLaughlin that the "Home for Historical Orphans in Washington" project was progressing, happily planned with separate residence halls for men and women, and a common lounge for intellectual discussions. Again funds failed to materialize, and with American entry into World War I the project was indefinitely postponed.[15]

Still Jameson did not give up, although in the absence of funds he made his program more modest by eliminating the idea of a student residence. In 1921, he again headed a planning committee, and the following year an announcement was made listing members of a "Board of Research Advisers"—each of them "having special familiarity with a given body of material"—who would be happy to "receive, protect, and advise" any students who requested their guidance. When students displayed no interest in this drastically narrowed project, Jameson publicized it with announcements to the various colleges' history departments as well as a notice in *The American Historical Review*. Aid in locating and gaining access to materials, he pointed out, was "no small matter in the archival confusion of Washington"; the members of the Board of Research Advisers were "earnestly desirous" of giving such assistance "to the utmost of their power" to "increasing numbers" of students. He urged any young scholar who contemplated a research excursion to Washington to apply by letter to the Bureau, enclosing his dean's written approval of the subject for study.[16] Students remained indifferent.

At the very moment of discouragement, however, two circumstances combined to give Jameson an opportunity to try, although on a limited scale, his plan as originally conceived. The wealthy Miss Shirley Farr of Vermont, who had worked under him at Chicago and who had relinquished her instructorship there to come to Carnegie for fifteen months on the staff of *The American Historical Review*,[17] agreed heartily with her director, Jameson, that the research and other advantages of Washington should somehow be made available to history students. Desirous also of advancing the professional status of her sex, she told Jameson in 1924 that should he hear of a young woman who would benefit from a year of study in Washington, she would be glad to finance her. Immediately Jameson began seeking a "crackerjack" woman student, and soon assured Miss Farr that he had found one. They then went to work on the details of what was to be to the close of his life an annual fellowship for women. Miss Farr wrote regarding the amount of the grant, "My idea is enough to live on without worry, but not to save money on; the increment should be purely scholastic." The two planners agreed upon a list of departments to which an annual request for candidates should go, and Jameson composed a form letter stating qualifications.[18]

The second advantageous circumstance was the establishment in Washington for the fields of political science and history of precisely the kind of student center that Jameson had envisioned for history. Robert S. Brookings, whom Jameson characterized as the "chief angel of Washington University, St. Louis," had provided funds to establish an institution in Washington devoted to research of value to American government. One department was to be a center for graduate students, who would receive board and a stipend as well as professional guidance. Brookings purchased two houses on I Street, N.W., as separate residences for the men and women, and scarcely had the house for women been acquired before Jameson, through his friendship with a Brookings staff member from Amherst, gained permission for the holder of his "feminine fellowship," as he called it, to rent a room there. The first incumbent later commented that "one of the most stimulating aspects of the winter was the arrangement which allowed me to live at the Brookings School where I enjoyed the utmost freedom of participating in the intellectual and social life."[19] Only on those occasions when the women fellows there were of sufficient number to fill all the accommodations did the history fellows fail to live at Brookings. Even then they enjoyed guest privileges.

Jameson was delighted that after so many years of effort he could bring at least one history student each year to enjoy Washington's rich advantages. He looked forward to arranging a meeting between the first fellow and her benefactor, but Miss Farr assured him unequivocally that she preferred to remain anonymous.[20] The grant soon came to be known as the "Jameson Fellowship," and Miss Farr regarded this designation as eminently fitting; she believed it one means of giving recognition to Jameson's contributions to the field of history.[21]

Jameson's attitude to the history fellows was perhaps a reflection of his sense of obligation to the donor. "I appreciate your public spirit and generosity," he wrote to Miss Farr. "It is a most intelligent way in which to spend money, and with my anxiety to have the advantages of Washington for historical work more fully known and used, it is one of the most encouraging things that has happened to me there. You can rely on my taking especial pleasure in helping whoever is so fortunate as to obtain the opportunity." And to the proponent of a candidate he wrote, "I feel anxious that the anonymous lady who gives the fellowship should feel rewarded by highly excellent work . . . and by good development and success afterward."[22]

This feeling of obligation easily communicated itself to the fellows; Jameson's serious tone with them was a clear indication that he expected full advantage to be taken of Washington's research opportunities. This impression, added to the impact of Jameson's dignified appearance, manner, and speech, as well as his stately carriage, might well lead the awestruck fellow to conclude after her first interview with him that her task was indeed a formidable one. Any feeling of fearfulness, however, would soon be dispelled by the comfortable academic atmosphere of the great high-domed room that constituted the Manuscript Division in the main building of the Library of Congress, and by the consistent helpfulness of the staff members, who brought the materials she needed to the tremendous round desk at the room's center. Soon she would realize that Jameson's daily nod as he passed from his glass-enclosed office was a friendly one, and would feel the genuine warmth of attitude beneath the frosty exterior.

Jameson, indeed, was sincere in his assurance to Miss Farr that he would always try to be helpful to the fellows. Although an important qualification of his form letter was the ability to follow lines of research "without much guidance," and although he told the proponent of one candidate that he could himself undertake "nothing more than that general giving of advice and suggestions from time to time which I am always happy to do in the case of any student that comes here,"[23] he was nevertheless always cordially interested in the fellow's progress, and always willing to suggest leads for further research. And if, as was usually the case, the fellowship year concluded the young woman's academic training, Jameson exercised his powerful influence to help her obtain a position. In the case of the last fellow to know him,[24] Jameson graciously extended the period of the grant when he learned that completion of manuscript research for her doctoral dissertation would take an additional month.

It was a characteristic gesture. Jameson's careful but cordial management of Miss Farr's grant is an indication that had he ever been able to realize his more elaborate plan he might have become, in addition to his other responsibilities, the able director of a Washington center that would have given resident students stimulation and experience to the benefit, as he hoped, of the entire field of history.

NOTES

[1] J. Franklin Jameson to Francis A. Christie, March 7, 1903, Jameson Papers, Manuscript Division, Library of Congress.

[2] Jameson to Daniel Coit Gilman, Feb. 14, 1902, *ibid.*

[3] Jameson to Mary W. Williams, April 4, 1924, *ibid.*

[4] American Historical Association, *Annual Report . . . 1901* (Washington, D. C., 1902), I, 41.

[5] Jameson to Francis A. Christie, March 7, 1903, Jameson Papers; Jameson, "The University Center for Research in Washington," *American Historical Review*, XXVIII, no. 2 (January, 1923), 259-62, p. 259.

[6] Jameson to Clarence W. Bowen, October 5, 1901; Bowen to Jameson, October 23, 1901, Jameson Papers.

[7] McLaughlin to Jameson, December 9, 1901; January 13, 1902, *ibid.* Miss Salmon's hope for a school in Rome was to be realized; it received a hundred thousand dollars from J. Pierpont Morgan, and in 1905 was chartered by Congress. *An Historian's World: Selections from Correspondence of John Franklin Jameson*, ed. Elizabeth Donnan and Leo F. Stock (Philadelphia, 1956), 81 n.

[8] Jameson to Francis A. Christie, November 24, 1901; February 15, 1902, *ibid.*

[9] Jameson to Gilman, February 14, 1902, *ibid.*

[10] Waldo G. Leland, "Memorandum for the Committee on Policy, September 1920," American Historical Association, *Annual Report . . . 1920* (Washington, D. C., 1925), 73-82, p. 81.

[11] "My talent, if I know myself, lies in the direction of Heuristik, and I thought I had shown this to the historical world and also the necessary ability to get other men to co-operate in historical tasks. . . ." Jameson to Christie, February 15; March 6, 1902, Jameson Papers.

[12] McLaughlin to Jameson, April 2, 1903, *ibid.* See also his letter to Jameson, June 11, 1902, *ibid.*

[13] McLaughlin to Jameson, April 2, 1903, *ibid;* American Historical Association, *Annual Report . . . 1920*, p. 81. McLaughlin did manage to bring a few students to Washington for brief periods of research. *An Historian's World*, 13.

[14] Jameson, "The University Center for Research in Washington," *op. cit.*, 259.

[15] *Ibid.*, 260; Jameson to McLaughlin, May 22, November 20, 1916, Jameson Papers; American Historical Association, *Annual Report . . . 1920*, Pp. 72, 81.

[16] Jameson, "The University Center for Research in Washington," *op. cit.*, 261; American Historical Association, *Annual Report . . . 1922* (Washington, D. C., 1926), I, 59.

[17] Walter Gibert to Jameson, March 29, 1922; Shirley Farr to

Jameson, December 18, 1921, Jameson Papers; Carnegie Institution, Department of Historical Research, *Year Book,* XX (Washington, D. C., 1921), 179; *ibid.,* XXI (Washington, 1922), 181; Harold G. Moulton to writer, October 28, 1963; Walter G. Leland's recollections in a conversation with the writer, October, 1963.

[18] Jameson to John S. Bassett, May 20, 28; June 4, 1924; Bassett to Jameson, May 26, 1924; Jameson to Shirley Farr, June 4, 1924; Farr to Jameson, June 2, 1924; carbon copy of a form-letter fellowship announcement, May 8, 1928, Jameson Papers.

[19] Jameson to Farr, August 12, 1924; Jameson to Mildred Stahl, August 29, 1924; Jameson to Waldo G. Leland, April 30, 1936; Jameson to Janet Woodburn, May 26, 1927; Stahl to Jameson, July 29, 1925, *ibid.*

[20] Farr to Jameson, June 2, 1924; Jameson to Farr, September 26, 1924; Stahl to Jameson, July 29, 1925, *ibid.*

[21] Waldo G. Leland's recollections in a conversation with the writer, October, 1963.

[22] Jameson to Farr, July 3, 1924; Jameson to David S. Muzzey, May 9, 1925, Jameson Papers.

[23] Carbon copy of form-letter fellowship announcement, May 8, 1928; Jameson to Bassett, May 28, 1924, *ibid.*

[24] This was the writer. Her successor did not have the opportunity of knowing Jameson, since he died the following autumn.

DR. JAMESON'S OTHER SIDE:
A PERSONAL MEMOIR

by Curtis W. Garrison

Dr. Jameson was a living monument. His rock-ribbed austere character and lifelong unsurpassed service to scholarship are recorded in many minds and places. It seems a bit audacious, then, after twenty-five years, while still under his influence, to write about the other Dr. Jameson, about his constant pleasantries, his foibles, his appreciation of the ridiculous, and his great heart. Those of us in the Library of Congress Manuscript Division who experienced his humor and warmth teetered between two poles—Dr. Jameson, the scholarly eminence, and Dr. Jameson, the very human person. Seldom could we lose sight of the first, but we nevertheless felt comforted by his presence. We were unhappy that all who knew him could not feel this.

Though his ancestry and New England rearing reined his feelings, the heart was not submerged. It was accessible. In a back-slapping, "first-name" world he seemed aloof. No one could take "liberties." It has recently been told that General Marshall was aghast when President Roosevelt during a war conference called him "George." The President sensed this and never did again. The same incident might have happened to Dr. Jameson, though it is very doubtful that Roosevelt could ever have been inspired to such familiarities with him. These feelings reflected a deep-rooted conviction of the dignity of man. Most New England Brahmins, many Southerners and many Philadelphians acted in this manner. It was not an arrogant forbidding facade, and Dr. Jameson's friendly nature shone through it to many persons, even on short acquaintance.

I shall never forget my first meeting with him. He was then Director of the Department of Historical Research in Carnegie Institution. A member of his staff had told me that they were in process of publishing the Jackson Papers and that these could be made available in page-proof form. Since this loan would aid my dissertation considerably, I called Dr. Jameson's secretary and she made arrangements for me to pick up the proofs one evening after work. On arrival at the office I found that Dr. Jameson was alone. I introduced myself—a fledgling close to first launching into flight. Though terribly awed, like most younger folk who first met him, I felt no apprehension. "Oh yes," he said. That was all. He then picked up the bulky proofs together with paper and string, and proceeded to wrap them up in a methodical, workmanlike manner. There was something unseemly to me in this eminence performing the menial task for a lowly student. "Let me do this," I interposed. "No, no," he said. So I stood and watched until he had it tied. His motions were unhasty, as always, and completely matter-of-fact. He did not wrap the proofs as though he were making a grand gesture. Whatever the job before him was, he did it. That was all. If Mrs. Pierce, his secretary, had been there, she might have done it. This scene, symbolically, was repeated many times during our association in after years.

This incident occurred during the winter at the beginning of 1928. By the following summer we had learned that Dr. Jameson was appointed Chief of the Library of Congress Manuscript Division, and was due to arrive early in the fall. He was also the first occupant of the newly-endowed Benjamin Chair of American History. It was assumed that his great abilities would be employed in laying down policies, in planning historical and archival projects, and in executive undertakings. Details of operations in the Manuscript Division, it was assumed, would be left to his chief assistant and to the meager staff. These thoughts showed our complete ignorance of Dr. Jameson's methods. He did launch into the policy and planning indicated. Amazingly, he also supervised our operations in great detail. On the first day of his ten years among the Manuscript Division staff, after a conference with his Assistant Chief, he emerged from his glass-bowl office and proceeded slowly from one desk to the other to greet each one and obtain from each a brief statement as to his duties. His approach to my desk always gave me the impression of a proud frigate bearing majestically down on a small craft. The noble Brahmin head set off by the intimate beard (the beard and face seemed as though born together), the proud blue eyes, the erect carriage, have ever been stamped on my memory.

> The front of Jove himself. . . .
> to give the world assurance of a man.

I had long been fearful on the outcome of my first encounter. He asked me the dreaded question—where did I receive my degree? I told him and he was very pleased, for he had his degree—in fact one of the first granted by that institution in the field of History—from the same university. Why was I afraid? I knew that many years before, during a long-forgotten struggle that rent The American Historical Association in two, my professor had been on the opposite side from him. Dr. Jameson was proud of the University and of his degree. I was his fellow-alumnus. He had obviously forgotten our brief meeting of the winter before.

Let me hasten to say that our mutual bond had no effect on him when he dealt with my colleagues on the Manuscript Division staff. Dr. Jameson's lines of authority ran from himself to each one individually. He never delegated his authority. There was great headshaking over his methods in the Library's executive offices, but not, however, by Dr. Putnam, the Librarian, who gave him full rein to run the Division in any manner he saw fit. The chief administrative

officer of the Library gave voice to this stricture and said,
"Dr. Jameson is undoubtedly a great scholar but he does
not know how to run a division." That pronouncement was
first made when he went on a trip (his Assistant Chief
being away at the time) expecting us to carry on the work
with which he had well loaded us before departing. However, new problems arose and we had to refer them to the
head office. Dr. Jameson rectified this administrative lapse
when he returned by designating one of the staff as "in
charge" should such a contingency again occur.

I did not see anything wrong at the time with Dr. Jameson's administrative methods since he remembered every
detail of our current tasks and kept well ahead of each
individual's work. We all worked harder for him than we
would have worked for any supervisor he might have interposed. We received authoritative answers to our queries.
We each had well-defined areas of work and we guarded our
provinces jealously. We might question, at times, our colleagues' methods but we never dared raise such questions
to the Chief. There was so much work to be done at the time
that our provinces did not overlap, though the lists and
indexes that some of us produced were made for general
Division use. Dr. Jameson coordinated all this work effort-
lessly even though the staff increased within five years from
four, when he first appeared on the scene, to about fourteen.
One of the by-problems of Dr. Jameson's direct-method administration was the consequent plight of the Assistant
Chief. When Dr. Jameson was away he became Acting Chief,
but even in summer when he was gone nearly three months
(all Washington executives ran away from the tropical heat
in those halcyon days), Dr. Jameson directed some of our
work, giving us special tasks by letter from his summer
home at North Edgecombe, Maine, and having bundles of
correspondence sent thither. He tried to solve the problem
by giving his Assistant Chief special jobs in ferreting out
manuscript collections and like assignments; but even so
this often left him for long periods spinning like a fifth
wheel.

In that first interview I remember telling him that I did not have enough to do, and he replied, "This state of affairs is entirely unnecessary. There is plenty of work for everybody." Every large depository usually has more than enough to busy any staff in arranging, describing, listing, cataloguing, shifting and boxing. We soon became aware of this, but in addition to these routine jobs, Dr. Jameson created masses of work by his mere presence and boundless energy. I wished at the time that I (age twenty-five) had the capabilities of work that he then had at age seventy. New collections began pouring in. These were the interest from his wide investment in acquaintances with public leaders and men of affairs. Scholars, awakened to the presence in the Division of the acknowledged Dean of historians, began writing long letters which entailed days and weeks in searches and listings for their reference. Dr. Jameson's contacts also included all the important dealers and collectors as well as the major historical societies and archives. These people trusted him to photostat their treasures, often in return for Library of Congress holdings. And the time-honored questions about Lincoln's *Gettysburg Address,* the *Ulster Gazette,* Washington's *Farewell Address,* the First Thanksgiving Proclamation, and many others seemed to increase.

Every question and project had to receive the same scrupulous service. One day when he handed me a letter written by a semi-literate person, I asked him why we should "bother" to reply with such care. He fixed me with his eye and replied, "This man is a taxpayer seeking knowledge from his Government. He deserves to be served in the same spirit in which he has written us."

And so our little band served him, and through him our citizens and our Government. Some of the band were not as impressed by him as others, as, for instance, the boy from the Middle West named Joe. Dr. Jameson's sense of propriety at times got the better of him, and he told Joe one day that he felt it would be more dignified, considering his position in such an important institution, if he were called "Joseph." Joe replied that he was christened "Joe" and that was the way it would have to be. On retiring from this conference, Joe was as red as a beet to have so rebuffed the august presence. Dr. Jameson, after this encounter, accepted Joe as the honest, strong character he undoubtedly was. He never allowed such contretemps to influence him. Joe later became a highly-respected professor in a mid-west university. Completely in contrast to Joe, a lady colleague at first could not overcome her awe-struck feelings of Dr. Jameson when she found she had to consult him. She would approach his office and just could not make it, withdrawing to summon up new courage. After some months his calm benignity assured her and her fears were allayed.

Those who did not know Dr. Jameson would never understand how he detested shallow pomposity. Some researchers worked for such long periods at desks in little cubicles of the Division that they were often mistaken for the staff. One of these, a very lovely young lady, was startled one day to see a volume hurtle from the second-tier stacks, narrowly missing her. Looking up to the balcony she recognized a well-known professor, and was about to get up to hand the book to him, when he said peremptorily, "Young lady! Bring that up to me at once!"

"You can go to hell!" she replied.

"I shall report you immediately!" he retorted, and stalked off.

Now we all knew this normally sweet-tempered researcher had considerable spirit and independence, and Dr. Jameson was not surprised at her natural indignation. Not many minutes later he drifted by her desk, grinning. He tapped her affectionately on the shoulder and said, "By Jove! I'm glad you said it!"

Dr. Jameson no doubt had to soothe the pompous professor's feathers, but his most amazing tact and diplomacy was called forth to solve the case of Dr. John C. Fitzpatrick, a volatile but fun-loving gentleman with the traditional Irish temperament. Dr. Fitzpatrick was the outstanding George Washington authority. Shortly before Dr. Jameson's advent he had been for some years the Assistant Chief of the Manuscript Division. When he heard of the new dispensation he felt that he deserved a raise to a special position of some kind instead of continuing, perhaps to the end of his career, in the same job. The Librarian could not see his point of view, and when Dr. Jameson arrived he found to his dismay that the Library's chief authority on manuscript work and the Library's collections had resigned. Dr. Fitzpatrick had a cubby-hole nearby and was attempting to organize "free-lance" research work for himself, assisted by Mrs. Fitzpatrick. From the recesses of his office he would glare at us whenever we would approach him for assistance. With consumate gentleness and helpful connections Dr. Jameson succeeded in winning him over. He assisted in his application for the full-time job as Editor of the bicentennial edition of Washington's Writings, and arranged to have him serve concurrently as a consultant to the Division. Dr. Fitzpatrick's abundant good nature overcame his dog-in-the-manger attitude and he was considered practically as part of the staff.

His little daughter—a child of terror—used to ride a book truck up and down the aisle by pushing against the cases on either side with her little arms. One time she ran full-tilt into Dr. Jameson while he was absorbed in studying some papers. Neither her spirits nor his dignity were disturbed.

Dr. Jameson had two secretaries, one of whom had served the Division for many years. She was always seeking to be helpful and one day undertook to straighten the large untidy-looking masses of papers he kept on a table behind his desk. She did not realize what most of us had learned, that you should not initiate a project intimately connected with his work without consulting him. When he returned to his labors after her tidy arranging he said little but looked sterner than ever for some time. He immediately began re-sorting them into their accustomed admirable disorder, and the secretary thereafter kept her hands off. He used

to joke about these piles, telling me one time, "I have a
paper here pertinent to our discussion—I think I can re-
trieve it from the Jurassic Strata." Dr. Jameson's other
secretary was the embodiment of youthful physical pulchri-
tude known in those days as the Clara Bow type. Her passage through the Division gave all the male staff a lift and
excitement to the spirits. We wondered about this phe-
nomenon until we realized how remarkably and capably
this eighteen-year-old handled Dr. Jameson's masses of
sometime erudite dictation. He appreciated near-perfection
in anybody.

Ours was surely a strange collection of workers. Many
of us were in the custodial grades, adroitly made useful by
explicit direction, by careful job analysis, by constant over-
sight without infringing on our integrity, and by masterful
editing of work. His memory of the past and the present
was fabulous, probably his supreme asset for supervision.
His unremitting care was rewarded by our loyalty and
good work, and when at times we would grow lax, as youth
does, he reproved us by circular bulletins, saying that he
saw and heard a great deal more than we would suppose,
and to please pull ourselves together. How many hundreds
of persons, including a few in the Division, whom he helped
to find good jobs can never be accurately estimated. A
letter from Dr. Jameson was almost a passport to one.

One of the most exciting members of the Manuscript
Division staff was a Welshman, B.A., Oxoniensis, referred
to Dr. Jameson by a friend. The Welshman had to find a
job or he would be returned to England by the United States
Immigration Service. Dr. Jameson was a great lover of
things British. He had the lad go to Canada while he
arranged with the Librarian and the immigration authorities to put him on his staff. This lovely, impulsive character
worked for us two years, sometimes writing poetry during
slack hours. He was like a bird flitting about over the staid
collections, completely out of his element, but striving
mightily to earn the pay in his monthly envelope. Eventually

he returned to Wales to write plays on Welsh miners. For many years now he has been on the staff of the British Broadcasting Company.

There was no limit to Dr. Jameson's patience and forbearance. One of his staff told him one day he would like to take time off to go some little distance on a honeymoon. He gave his assent readily. Some days later, so I was told, Dr. Jameson approached him and said, "There has just come to my attention a manuscript collection that needs to be surveyed, and so I shall have to arrange for you to do it. By the way, its location is not far—in fact, on the way back from the spot you have selected for your honeymoon." So the Government was served by acquiring valuable knowledge on the important collection, and my friend had some of his honeymoon travel expenses liquidated. Dr. Jameson's innate modesty and retreat from the center of the stage whenever possible was beautifully illustrated at my friend's wedding. I was there, and Dr. Jameson, after the ceremony, was rapidly becoming the center of a circle which included my friend, the groom. The groom, wishing to show honor to the great man, said that now he felt the affair was complete—he was going to add, "with Dr. Jameson's presence." Dr. Jameson quickly interposed, saying, "Well, the ceremony is performed, the register signed, the clergyman is fed, and—yes! I presume the affair is *really* complete." All this in a matter-of-fact tone.

One secret of Dr. Jameson's unusual success with his staff was his love of youth. Most of the staff were under thirty and some of them under twenty-five. Like all creative, mentally energetic, vital persons he felt that youth, in their exuberance, held the future. He appreciated the natural attraction between those of opposite sex and the importance of keeping the race of man going on this earth. He was amazed therefore at Benjamin Franklin's blasé conception of the mistress which he noted one day after showing an important visitor our copy of the Bagatelles. Pointing to this document he said to me with some indignation, "He does not think the

age of the mistress is of importance!" Youth or relative age
equality made the great difference between just sex and love
in his mind.

And he was not afraid of the nation's youth. They seemed
safe from prevalent 'isms' to him. Apropos of this he used
to remark: "The most popular magazine among the youth
of the country is the *Saturday Evening Post*. This statistic
completely destroys the argument of those who fear the
subversion of the country's youth to Communism."

His helpfulness and sympathy for youth were illustrated
one evening when we heard a loud banging on the Manuscript Division door after the Division had been closed and
locked up for the day. I was alone with him, doing some extra
work until he should depart, no one being allowed there after
hours unless in his company. Dr. Jameson walked with his
usual slow pace to the door and unlocked it. The excited
voice of a student from Cuba was heard, imploring Dr.
Jameson to lend him ten dollars. This student had made quite
a splash about the Library and in the Division at times during the preceding two weeks. He told Dr. Jameson that he
must catch a train to New York in thirty minutes and various circumstances had prevented him from drawing on his
account. Dr. Jameson, without a word, pulled out his wallet
and produced the bill, said, "Not at all, not at all," to the
protestations of gratitude, locked the door and walked back
to his office. He was only slightly acquainted with the man!
"Do you think you will ever see that again?" I asked. "Oh
yes,"he replied, and went on with his work.

So Dr. Jameson proceeded through this life steadily and
unhurriedly, building up our great manuscript collection, assisting thousands of scholars, writing thousands of letters
on scores of subjects, advising on statesmanlike projects
such as the *Dictionary of American Biography*, serving and
passing the time of day with those who crossed his path.
Would that I had noted the scores of anecdotes, both historical and mundane, with which he often regaled us. Alas!
How blind not to have realized their intimate interest in a
later day.

I remember only one, and also a favorite saying. The two juxtaposed represent, I think, his philosophy of living. The story concerns an uncle in the Massachusetts town of his boyhood. The uncle kept a general store, and it seems one morning he missed a barrel of molasses. He kept this information to himself, however, and weeks passed without trace of the theft. One day one of the group around the cracker barrel suddenly asked, "John, did you ever catch the man who took that barrel of molasses?" "Yes, I have," said the uncle; "Now you can pay me!"

The favorite saying has appeared in one of his early articles, and he wrote it down in a letter to me in response to mine complaining of vicious gossip. "You worry too much, and are much too sensitive," he wrote. "I always liked the Scottish saying, 'They say. What say they? Let them say.'"

He himself kept his counsel until he believed it might be effective and so served his fellowman.

J. FRANKLIN JAMESON AND THE ATLAS OF THE HISTORICAL GEOGRAPHY OF THE UNITED STATES

by John K. Wright

In 1932, the Carnegie Institution of Washington and the American Geographical Society of New York jointly published a substantial volume containing 637 maps printed on 227 pages, and also 175 pages of letterpress.[1] The product of many years of scholarly research and craftsmanship, this *Atlas of the Historical Geography of the United States* stands as a monument both to Dr. Jameson and to its principal author, the late Dr. Charles O. Paullin. Jameson conceived the first plans for it and supervised the work that produced the greater part of its contents. For this reason, although his name is not on the title page, it seems only fitting to refer to the *Atlas* in this essay as the "Jameson-Paullin" atlas, and I am sure that Dr. Paullin would have warmly approved my doing so.

The seeds of a later interest in historical geography could well have been planted in the young Jameson's mind while he was a graduate student at The Johns Hopkins University. In 1881, he borrowed E. A. Freeman's *Historical Geography of Europe* from the library to read in preparation for auditing a course of lectures by Freeman. At first he found the lecturer "inexpressibly dull," then "good," and finally "excellent." President Daniel Coit Gilman and the historian,

Professor Herbert B. Adams, were aiming to build up geographical collections and instruction in geography in the University as aids to the postgraduate study of history. Adams had geographical leanings, and Gilman was something of a geographer, for he had served during his earlier years as professor of geography at Yale and even for a few months in 1860, as General Secretary of the American Geographical and Statistical Society (as it was then called).

Gilman and Adams assigned Jameson two jobs that he seems to have taken on somewhat reluctantly, to judge from his diary and letters. One was "arranging the bureau of maps" and the other, lecturing on "the relation of physical geography to history." Arnold Guyot of Princeton was then the leading professor of geography in this country and possibly the only one, since Gilman had become an administrator. In the spring of 1883, Jameson went to Princeton to consult Guyot about this first chore, but unfortunately Guyot was ill, and the younger man had to make do with what he could learn from the professor's assistants. On returning to Baltimore, Jameson "spent considerable time making lists of books to be purchased, examining maps, and planning a room for the new bureau," a room which Adams described not long after as containing, among other things, "conveniently catalogued maps, charts, diagrams, etc., of physical and historical geography."

Jameson was none too well prepared for the second chore, which he had to perform the next year. In January, 1884, he wrote his father: "Oh, those fearful, fearful lectures! They haunt me day and night, especially this first one. After that one, perhaps it won't be so bad," and it wasn't. Miss Elizabeth Donnan has noted, however, that although "his lamentations" over the lectures "were frequent, he grew somewhat more interested before the term was over." In a report of *The Study of History in American Colleges and Universities* (1887), Adams wrote: "in the Johns Hopkins University, physical and historical geography were made the basis of instruction in historical and political science." The report also shows clearly that in the eighties, in other

American centers, more and more attention was being paid
to historical geography. Jameson's interest in it, however,
was not awakened until some twenty years later.

While a professor at the University of Chicago, he read
in the paper one day that Dr. Gilman had been elected the
first president of the new Carnegie Institution of Washington. So, on February 14, 1902, he sent Gilman "a lot
of suggestions" as to what the Institution "might do for
history." One was that it should produce "a really first-rate
atlas of American historical geography." He explained that
this was "a great desideratum," a book which "no publisher
could afford to prepare because most of the maps would require a large and expensive amount of pioneer research
work," and a calculation shows that about half of the maps
in the *Atlas* (or, strictly speaking, pages devoted to maps)
must have actually required such expensive, time-consuming
research in their compilation. These are the maps—notably
in the sections devoted to population, churches, boundaries,
lands, and political votes—that give the *Atlas* its unusual
distinction among works of its kind and that have won the
greatest praise from discriminating reviewers.

Later in 1902, when planning a course on the "auxiliary
sciences" of history, Jameson asked Professor G. L. Burr
of Cornell for advice. The first ten lectures were to be
devoted to "historical geography, or, more broadly, to the
use of geography for the benefit of history. I know that you
have conducted a formal course in historical geography,"
Jameson wrote, "and I do not know of any other man in
the country who has." In replying at some length, Burr
distinguished carefully between (1) "what Ratzel has
christened 'Anthropo-geography,'" (2) "the yet more important, though neglected influence of man on the earth"—
he mentioned Marsh and Hahn in this connection, and (3)
"what I count Historical Geography proper (the geography
which was present geography to *past* ages)." Burr explained
that he had his students investigate the last-named subject
"both statistically and dynamically — *das Sinn und das
Wesen*—epoch-wise and in development."

I have not tried to ascertain whether Burr's letter influenced Jameson's lectures or whether the latter in any way foreshadowed the plan for an atlas that Jameson drew up a little over a year later. The important point in relation to the *Atlas*, however, is that Burr and Jameson were both Historians, and hence their concern was with historical geography as an "auxiliary science" to History, the capital letters here being used to differentiate, respectively, the "discipline" of History and its devotees, on the one hand, from what had happened in the past, and those who investigate such happenings, on the other.

Ever since, the Revival of Learning researches in historical geography have been pursued as adjuncts to History —at first to Ancient and Biblical History, and later to Military, National, European, and World History, and to the History of Civilization. The Jameson-Paullin *Atlas* is a product of this time-hallowed tradition. Dr. Jameson, who planned and supervised it, Dr. Paullin, who did more work on it than anyone else, and its editor had all received doctor's degrees in History, and historians dug out most of the information that it sets forth. Geographers have also devoted themselves to historical geography but, except for Dr. Isaiah Bowman, Professor R. H. Whitbeck, the editor (a renegade Historian), and a few others, geographers had little to do with the making of the *Atlas*. In 1932 the young profession of geography in the United States could not have produced a historical atlas of the United States of the magnitude and scholarly quality of the Jameson-Paullin *Atlas,* and probably it could not do so today—which is not meant to imply that the historians have a monopoly in historical geography or that there is not merit in geographers' seeking to develop the subject independently.

On November 3, 1903, Dr. Jameson wrote from the University of Chicago to Dr. Andrew C. MacLaughlin,[2] his predecessor as the head of the Department of Historical Research at the Carnegie Institution. The plan for the *Atlas* outlined in this letter (Appendix I) might be likened to a simplified drawing of an embryo in its early stages of

development. Nearly everything was there that was eventually to emerge full-formed into the light of day, though
much of it different in size and shape. Jameson recommended
"seven varieties of maps," for five of which he gave additional detailed suggestions, amounting to a total of some
forty-five specific items that he felt should be covered.

In the *Atlas* (p. xi), there is a table giving totals and percentages regarding the amount of space on which maps are
printed. The maps are classed in two major groups, each
having six lesser categories. The text explains that the maps
in the first major category, which account for more than
half of the space, deal in the main with the chronicle of the
material expansion of the American nation across the
continent: "the story of the exploration and charting of
mountains, rivers, lakes, and plains, of the spreading tide
of settlement into vacant lands; of friendly and hostile contacts between settlers and Indians; of the progress of settlement as it was fostered here and thwarted there by the
great facts of nature; of the use made of natural resources;
of the apportioning of land among individuals; of the ad-
justment of political claims to territory; and of the marking
out of new administrative units." By contrast, the maps of
the second major category relate predominantly to the
economic, political, cultural, and military history of the
country—as developed subsequently to the dates of first
settlement.

Table I, herewith, shows the contents of the *Atlas* as
classified in the same manner as in the table in the *Atlas,*
except that in Table I the topics are arranged more nearly
in accordance with the order in which they actually appear
in the *Atlas*. Table I also sheds light on the degree to which
the work was done, respectively, at the Carnegie Institution
of Washington (and hence under Dr. Jameson's inspiration
and supervision) up to 1927, and at the American Geographical Society between 1929 and 1932; and also on the degree
to which the *Atlas* as a whole and its several parts consist
of reproductions as distinguished from maps that were made
especially for the purpose. In addition, it gives references

to the items in Dr. Jameson's plan of 1903, which gave rise to, or at least foreshadowed, corresponding parts of the *Atlas*. By comparing the Table with the plan it will be seen that Jameson's proposed maps classed "A" (Physical),

TABLE I—*Atlas of the Historical Geography of the United States*

	Number of maps[1] (1)	Totals % (2)	Supplied by		Reproductions (5)	Made especially for *Atlas* from	
			C.I.W. (3)	A.G.S. (4)		Statistics (6)	Other data (7)
Natural environment [A][3]	32	4.0	1.5	2.5	0.4		3.6
Cartography and explorers' routes [B]	50	16.8	16.5	0.3	15.5		1.3
Indians [C:1, 6]	10	3.1	2.7	0.4	5.8		3.1
Lands [C:2-7; D:12]	57	11.9	9.9	2.0			6.1
Settlement and population [D:1-5]	79	12.1	10.1	2.0		12.1	
Boundaries [C:4, 8]	40	8.4	8.1	0.3			8.4
Total	268	56.3	48.8	7.5	21.7	12.1	22.5
Churches, colleges, universities [D:6]	36	5.1	5.1				5.1
Political maps [E]	72	12.3	12.1	0.2			12.3
Reform movements [D:11]	38	6.2	5.2	1.0			6.2
Agriculture, transportation, manufacturers, commerce [D:7-10]	156	13.5	9.5	4.0	2.8	10.7	
Plans of cities [G]	7	2.2	2.0	0.2	2.2		
Military history, etc. [F; C:11]	60	4.4		4.4			4.4
Total	369	43.7	33.9	9.8	5.0	10.7	28.0
Grand totals	637	100	82.7	17.3	26.7	22.8	50.5

[1] Since the maps differ so greatly in size (varying from less than 1 sq. in. to approximately 225 sq. in.), these figures are less significant than those in cols. 2–7.

[2] Maps are printed on approximately 25,300 sq. in. of paper surface in the *Atlas*. The figures in cols. 2–7 show percentages of this total. One full plate (i.e., printed on two pages of one leaf) has an area of approximately 225 sq. in., or a little less than 1% of the total map surface.

[3] References in [ ] are to Dr. Jameson's letter of November 5, 1903 (Appendix I).

"B" (Cartography and Discovery), "E" (Political Facts), "F" (Events, such as campaigns and battles), and "G" (Towns) have similar counterparts in the *Atlas*, whereas his proposals for "C" (Boundaries and Subdivisions) are reflected in the three parts of the *Atlas* devoted to "Lands, etc.," "Boundaries," and "Indians," and those for "D" (Social facts and developments) are represented in the sections of the *Atlas* devoted to "Settlement and Population" and to economic, political, cultural, and military history.

In 1905, Dr. Jameson succeeded Dr. MacLaughlin as Director of the Department of Historical Research of the Carnegie Institution, and he served in this capacity until 1928. The progress of further planning for and work upon the *Atlas* may be followed through 1927 in his annual reports, and with the subsequent events is summarized thus in the Introduction to the *Atlas:*

> The making of the *Atlas* was authorized by the Carnegie Institution of Washington in 1911, and work was begun the following year when Dr. Paullin was employed for four months on a survey of possibilities and on other preliminary tasks. In 1913, he was placed in charge and from 1914 until 1927, gave all his time to the work, with the exception of a few intermissions caused by the World War and other exigencies. He was aided by numerous scholars of history and geography whose names and services are, for the most part, mentioned in the Preface. [The Preface, by Dr. Paullin, names forty or more persons who "aided him," including several of the leading American historians of the period—notably Turner, Libby, Farrand, Robertson, and Jernegan.]

> In order that the *Atlas* might be further strengthened geographically and might benefit from the experience and technical skill of the American Geographical Society in editing and publishing maps, an arrangement was made in 1929, whereby the Society accepted the responsibility of bringing the enterprise to a close. Besides editing and seeing the publication through

the hands of lithographer, printer, and binder,
the Society has rearranged the material and has
added, with the approval of the Carnegie Institution, a considerable number of new maps [see
Table I, Col. (4)] with corresponding text.

The materials for the *Atlas* as prepared at the Carnegie
Institution had been designed with a view to the production
of a larger and more expensive volume than was the *Atlas*
as finally published. Dr. Isaiah Bowman, Director of the
American Geographical Society when the Society assumed
responsibility for the *Atlas,* conceived the idea that only a
few maps would have to be sacrificed and that the general
utility of the volume might be greatly enhanced by reducing
the height and width of the pages by about a third and by
printing as many maps as possible back-to-back. This was
done, and it enabled the Society to get out the *Atlas* as a
handy volume that could be sold for fifteen dollars. The dis-
advantages due to the change in format are manifest in
departures from the optimum scales for a few of the maps
(the vast majority were published at the scales originally
contemplated) and in the illogical order in which certain
maps are arranged in the sections on "Cartography" and
on "Lands." The change also necessitated the rejection of
a number of early maps that were to have been included
in the section on "Cartography."

Except for a few minor details—for example, his suggestions that there should be maps of federal judicial districts, ecclesiastical dioceses, and "religions in their proportions to the total population"—the *Atlas* embodies the
essence of Dr. Jameson's entire plan of 1903, and about
nine-tenths of its contents in the form of maps reflect planning done by him or by Dr. Paullin or others under his
supervision. Although Table I indicates that the American
Geographical Society may be credited with the production
of the maps filling seventeen per cent of the space devoted
to maps in the *Atlas,* a considerable part of the work done
at the Society was in further prosecution of work planned
and begun before the Society took over the enterprise.

Comprehensive and suggestive as it was, Dr. Jameson's plan of 1903 bore the earmarks of its day. It reveals little or no evidence of awareness that the concept of "the historical geography of the United States" might include the study of areas outside the territorial limits of our country as of the period before the Spanish-American War. Insofar as his and Dr. Paullin's planning bore fruit in the materials for the *Atlas* prepared before 1929, the words "United States" in its title would seem to have meant an *area,* with its tangible and intangible contents, rather than a *nation.* When the American Geographical Society assumed responsibility for the *Atlas,* the United States had emerged as one of the most powerful and influential nations in the world. By that time it had become natural to construe the term "historical geography of the United States" as pertaining not only to what has existed and developed within our country's boundaries, but also to geographical aspects of the nation's external relations—physical, political, military, commercial, economic, cultural, and so forth. By adding a few maps the Society tried to recognize, if not to do full justice, to this broader view. The Society also added a number of other maps that seemed needed to make the *Atlas* a more generally useful tool than it might otherwise have been for students and the "general reader"—if not necessarily for mature scholars.

The *Atlas* was published in October, 1932, in an edition of 5600, and has not been reprinted. It went out of print in 1949.[3] Soon after its publication it was widely reviewed in the newspapers and in educational and scholarly journals. I have recently read some forty of the reviews, which range in length from a paragraph or two to an eight-page article in small print by Dr. Leopold G. Scheidl in the *Mitteilungen* of the Vienna Geographical Society. Most of the reviews, especially those for school teachers, librarians, and the "general reader," were laudatory or even ecstatic.

Those in the scholarly journals were more discriminating. They were divided about equally in numbers between historical magazines published mostly in this country, geographical magazines published mostly abroad, and a scattering of miscellaneous magazines devoted to science, political and social studies, and law. Several reviewers displayed their erudition by pointing out sins of omission—topics not treated in the *Atlas* or treated insufficiently, in the reviewers' opinion. Fewer were those who listed sins of commission— actual mistakes. Most of the reviewers either quoted from or paraphrased or summarized the Introduction (which describes the *Atlas* and explains how it was made), and a goodly proportion would even seem to have examined some of the maps and read some of the text. This, however, is not the place for a dissertation on the *mores* of reviewers.

One of the fairest and also severest was Frederick Merk in the *New England Quarterly*. He called certain of the maps "stupendous," "superlative," "magnificent"; and others he felt were "perfunctory," "erroneous," "misleading." (He considered the Index "unfortunately brief," fifteen pages as against ninety-four in Shepherd's *Historical Atlas;* the answer here is that there are more entries per page in the Jameson-Paullin index than in that of Shepherd, and that the maps in the latter's atlas are plastered with names, whereas most of those in Jameson-Paullin carry no names, and the majority of those that do so are reproductions of old maps on which most of the names have no historical significance.) Professor Merk, however, conceded that the *Atlas* merited the Loubat Prize of $1000, which it won in 1933. This prize is awarded every five years by Columbia University for the "best work" of the preceding quinquennium "printed and published in the English language on the History, Geography, Archeology, Ethnology, Philology, or Numismatics of North America." Dr. Jameson and Dr. Paullin would have found satisfaction in reading in *A Guide to the Study of the United States of America,* published by the Library of Congress in 1960, that "after 25 years" the *Atlas* "remains unrivaled," and also in knowing that a copy is among the books recently selected by a Committee of Librarians and others for inclusion in the President's Library at the White House.

NOTES

[1] *Atlas of the Historical Geography of the United States*, by Charles O. Paullin, Carnegie Institution of Washington; edited by John K. Wright, Librarian, American Geographical Society of New York. Published jointly by the Carnegie Institution of Washington and the American Geographical Society of New York, 1932. XV and 160 pp.; 166 plates of maps on 61 tipped-in leaves; 11 x 14½ in. (28 x 36½ cm.).

[2] Surname is more commonly spelled McLaughlin. MacLaughlin is here used throughout to conform with Jameson's letter in Appendix.

[3] Argosy-Antiquarian, Ltd., of New York City, is contemplating reprinting the *Atlas*.

NOTE ON SOURCES OF INFORMATION

The data in this study concerning the development of Dr. Jameson's interest in historical geography prior to 1904, are derived from certain of his letters and commentary on them in *An Historian's World: Selections from the Correspondence of John Franklin Jameson*, edited by Elizabeth Donnan anld Leo F. Stock (*Memoirs of the American Philosophical Society*, Vol. 42, Philadelphia, 1956). See also J. K. Wright, "Daniel Coit Gilman: Geographer and Historian," *Geographical Review*, Vol. 51, 1961, pp. 381-99; and, on historical and geographical studies at Johns Hopkins and elsewhere in the eighties, see H. B. Adams, "The Study of History in American Colleges and Universities," [U.S.] *Bureau of Education Circular No. 2*, Washington, 1887.

Progress at the Carnegie Institution of Washington in the planning and making of the *Atlas* may be followed in Dr. Jameson's reports as Director of the Department of Historical Research. These may be found in the *Yearbooks* of the Institution, Nos. 5, 1906, and 8-27, 1909-1928, copies of which were kindly sent to me by Mrs. G. P. Bauer of the Institution's staff. Dr. W. W. Ristow of the Library of Congress had been good enough to inform me that correspondence folders numbered 128, 129, and 130 in Box 11 of the "Papers of J. Franklin Jameson" in the Manuscript Division of the Library relate to the *Atlas*. Through Dr. Ristow's help I secured a photostatic copy of Jameson's letter to Dr. MacLaughlin, from which Appendix I has been copied.

My comments concerning the part taken by the American Geographical Society in the publication and distribution of the *Atlas* and concerning its subsequent reception are based partly on the Preface and Introduction to the *Atlas* itself, partly on personal recollections, and partly on information kindly furnished by Mrs. Dorothea Hanatschek of the American Geographical Society and by Miss Virginia Close of the Baker Library, Dartmouth. Table I is based partly on the table on page xi of the *Atlas,* but for the most part on a new analysis made by me in October, 1963.

APPENDIX I

5551 Lexington Avenue
Chicago

November 5, 1903.

J. Franklin Jameson
Professor of History in the
University of Chicago

My dear MacLaughlin:

I cheerfully offer such suggestions as I can make regarding an Atlas of the Historical Geography of the United States.

I suppose it would be agreed that there would be no point in the Carnegie Institution's undertaking such a thing unless it were to be made so elaborate in scope, so complete in point of scholarship, and therefore so expensive, that it could not be executed in any other way than through an endowment. Therefore, I will mention all the things which occur to me as desirable in an historical atlas of the United States, regardless of the fact that some of the maps proposed would require expensive researches never yet made. Yet, as the Carnegie Institution would probably wish that the product should be sold, not given away—sold perhaps at a price covering the mechanical execution —I mean to keep within the bounds of what is practicable on that basis.

I should think that an ideal atlas of the historical geography of the United States would include seven varieties of maps:

A. Physical

1. Maps exhibiting configuration and formation,—coasts, mountains and rivers.
2. A map or maps exhibiting the facts of climate.
3. A map or maps exhibiting mineral stores and the area covered by forests at certain dates.
4. Maps exhibiting the products or industries of different regions,— somewhat as in Vidal-Lablache.

    B. Maps illustrating the development of cartography, or, in a more general phrase, illustrating the progress of discovery. Whether a procedure so elaborate as that which Harrisse has

employed in the case of Newfoundland would be justifiable
I am not sure, but, by some combination of his methods and
the simpler ones employed by Winsor, it should be possible to
illustrate:

1. The early period of the discovery of America.
2. The gradual completion of knowledge of the Atlantic and Gulf
   coast lines.
3. The same for the Pacific coast.
4. The same for the lakes and the interior.

C. Maps illustrating boundaries and divisions:

1. The location of Indian tribes at the beginning of European
   settlement.
2. The claims of various European powers.
3. Grants by various European authorities,—including maps on
   which should be carried out in detail the various grants in New
   England, the Middle States, and the South, respectively.
4. Boundaries of colonies and their boundary disputes.
5. Maps showing the new states proposed between 1776 and 1787.
6. Maps showing at different periods the boundaries of states, territories, and Indian reservations.
7. Maps showing acquisitions by the United States.
8. Maps illustrating boundary disputes of the United States: N.E.,
   N.W., S.W., Texas, and Alaska.
9. A map or maps showing the federal judicial circuits and districts.
10. One showing ecclesiastical dioceses,—Catholic and Episcopal.
11. A map illustrating the processes of Secession and Reconstruction.

D. Maps illustrating social facts and developments, such as are
in the Statistical Atlas for the 11th Census. To this division
great attention should naturally be paid in the case of the
United States;—far greater than has even been paid in
European historical atlases.

1. Maps showing the location of early settlements, e.g., settlements
   in the colonies established before 1700, and settlements and posts
   in the West established before 1800.
2. Maps illustrating the growth of population.
3. Of colored population.
4. Maps showing nationality.
5. Maps exhibiting the location of natives of each State, as is done
   in Plates 23-31 of the Statistical Atlas; and so exhibiting the facts
   of migration.

6. Maps of religions, in their proportions to total population.
7. Maps showing the proportion to pop[ulation] of wage-earners in the great branches of industry.
8. Maps showing proportions of improved lands to areas.
9. Maps showing early routes, and also railroads and canals.
10. Maps showing for different periods the valuation per capita of different states or districts.
11. Maps related to the history of slavery, showing the amount and density of holdings, and the secessive steps in abolition.
12. Maps illustrating the history of the land policy of the United States government.

   E. Maps illustrating political facts: not only parties and elections, but the local attitudes on great questions, after the manner of Libby, A.H.A., 1896, 323-334.

   F. Maps illustrating events, such as campaigns and battles. This is such a stock variety that I need only mention it.

   G. Maps of towns, e.g., Boston, Philadelphia, Baltimore, and Charleston in 1775; New York in 1789; Philadelphia in 1800; Washington in 1814; Baltimore, Richmond, Charleston and New Orleans in 1861.

If these suggestions are of any good to you, I shall be very glad, and if the project advances further I shall always be very much interested in it.

Believe me,

Very truly yours,

(Signed) J. F. Jameson.

J. FRANKLIN JAMESON AND THE
DICTIONARY OF AMERICAN BIOGRAPHY

by Dumas Malone

From the time that the Committee of Management of the *Dictionary of American Biography* was appointed in 1924, until the completion of the original edition in 1936, J. Franklin Jameson was its chairman. Equally if not more important in the history of that great work of cooperative scholarship is the part he played in initiating the project and planning its course. If the brief account of the enterprise in Volume XX does not give him the full measure of credit he deserves, the fault may be attributed to his modesty and my failure to redress the balance. He and I collaborated in preparing that account, the first portion being largely written by him and the second by me. However, I had to exercise my editorial prerogatives with respect to his section, in the effort to keep him from minimizing his own services. He properly gave credit to other men, especially to Frederick Jackson Turner, who proposed at the first meeting of the American Council of Learned Societies and again at the second that the possibility of preparing such a work be looked into, and who rendered notable services as a member of the planning committee which the Council set up in 1922. But Dr. Jameson was chairman of that committee and had to admit that he procured the subvention of $500,000 from Adolph S. Ochs of the *New York Times* to meet the estimated cost of preparing the manuscript, though he claimed that this task was easy. The other members share the credit for the wise plans that were formulated—so wise that only minor deviations from them were ever necessary—but Dr. Jameson's influence was continuous and must have been very great. No finer tribute could be paid the published work than to say that it faithfully adhered to the principles laid down by his committee.

My understanding is that he was directly responsible for the happy choice of Allen Johnson as editor. Since I did not join the staff until more than three years later, I have no personal knowledge of the relations between these two men in the intervening period, but everything I saw and heard afterwards confirmed the impression that the conduct of the chairman of the Committee of Management was irreproachable. Having entrusted the conduct of the enterprise to such skillful hands, he scrupulously refrained from any sort of interference. He was always available for counsel, however, and in the early months, when the editor was creating an organization, drawing up the original list of names, and surveying the country for contributors, more consultation was needed than ever thereafter. I am sure that Dr. Jameson never gave gratuitous advice, but in view of his unrivaled knowledge of American historical scholarship and of the workers in all fields, his counsel could not have failed to be invaluable.

His confidence in the editor of his choosing was abundantly justified, but Dr. Johnson's interpretation of the catholicity which the planning committee had enjoined went somewhat further than Dr. Jameson appears to have anticipated. This forward-looking champion of learning who did so much to advance it was in matters of taste an old-fashioned gentleman. It is not surprising, therefore, that he was somewhat perturbed by the admission to the assemblage of American notables of athletes and dancers, along with occasional gamblers, freaks, and other bizarre characters. I doubt if, left to himself, he would have put some of these in, but he accepted all the editorial decisions with the best of grace and took great pride in the remarkable breadth of view which became so characteristic of the *Dictionary*. He loved to read the articles and I would not be surprised to learn that he got through nearly all of them.

The responsibility for selecting me as junior editor was that of Allen Johnson, and this may have been another instance of deference to the field commander on the part of Dr. Jameson. When I joined the organization I was in much awe of him. This was not merely because of the austerity which everybody saw in him at first glance, but because of the vastness of his knowledge and the incredible retentiveness and appalling precision of his mind. That it was also a notably judicious mind I soon found out, but, as I told Allen Johnson, I had an inferiority complex in this majestic presence. Whether or not my senior colleague meant what he said, he sought to reassure me by claiming that he did too. Even after I had grown a little older and assumed major responsibility for the enterprise, I continued to view the sage of American historical scholarship with diffidence, but this merged with reverence as time went on.

Actually, I did not see him very often. He was then chief of the Division of Manuscripts at the Library of Congress and I was nearly always grinding away in our offices in the Hill Building within a few blocks of the White House. From time to time I would call him up to ask his judgment about some matter of policy. As I well remember, I would say my piece and then be met by what seemed an inordinately long silence—long enough to set me wondering if I had presented the matter clumsily or unwittingly made some mistake. Then, after saying, "Well," he would make an unhurried, well-reasoned, and well-worded reply. I am sure he never wrote an imperfect sentence and I doubt if he ever uttered one. His omniscience was a great comfort to us in moments of uncertainty. Some of the reviews of the successive volumes contained lists of persons who *might* have been included. Many of these names we had actually considered and rejected, but others we had never heard of, and whenever we found that Dr. Jameson had not heard of them we felt relieved. Any American historical character he did not know about seemed not worth noticing.

One of those rare afternoons when I was out of the office and working in the Division of Manuscripts in the Library of Congress—then in the main building—I had hardly begun to realize that the daylight was growing dim when somebody leaned over and switched on the desk lamp. Turning, I saw Dr. Jameson standing tall and straight behind me, with a flicker of a smile on his face. This may now seem too small an incident to be worth recording, but it left an ineffaceable memory of his watchfulness and thoughtfulness. Somehow it symbolized his unending desire to facilitate all scholarship and to be of all possible help to any scholar. He was not only a master in the field but a father in the faith.

This was before Allen Johnson was stricken down by an automobile. That sad event revealed an affectionate, even a sentimental, side of Dr. Jameson's nature which many people may never have suspected in one so characteristically restrained. The first time I talked with him afterwards he was so choked with grief that he could hardly speak. At my request he wrote for the *Dictionary* a sketch of the man whose selection as editor had proved so fortunate and whose sudden death had so shocked us all. In its published form it is a model article in every respect, but originally it violated one of the principles that Dr. Jameson's own planning committee had laid down: it did *not* eschew sentiment. So he and I toned it down, knowing that the late editor himself would have preferred it so.

After I became sole editor early in 1931, Dr. Jameson treated me with the same respect he had shown my senior colleague, despite my relative immaturity. He would have been far more warranted in making unsolicited suggestions than he had been in Allen Johnson's time, but I cannot remember that he ever made one. Nor can I recall any word of criticism he ever uttered. We all knew that he expected us to maintain the highest standards, but somehow, despite the fact that I never quite got over my awe of him,

I never felt any hesitancy in telling him casually, even jokingly, about our mistakes. Being thoroughly familiar with the problems which confront all editors, he was always compassionate, and he by no means lacked a sense of humor. One came to take his sympathy and loyalty for granted.

I have long regarded J. Franklin Jameson as the most learned man in the field of history that I ever knew. It is regrettable that he did not write more, since he knew so much, thought so clearly, and wrote so well, but he was content to lay foundations on which other men—lesser men than he—could build. There was no arrogance in him, no thirst for glory. In his eyes it was the work of historical scholarship that counted. When with him, I always felt that I was in the presence of a truly great man, and I shall ever deem it an honor to have had a share in building something on a foundation that he firmly laid.

JOHN FRANKLIN JAMESON AND THE NATIONAL ARCHIVES

by Fred Shelley

The need for a national archives building had been felt by responsible administrators, chief clerks and others from time to time during the nineteenth century.[1] In the 1890's, preliminary plans were drawn. And in 1903, land was purchased[2] for a federal "Hall of Records," but "Nobody seemed to take interest enough to have the building put up. . . ." So wrote Elihu Root to Jameson some years later.[3]

A "Hall of Records" was envisioned as a large building in which generous storage spaces would be assigned to various agencies. Each agency would have retained direct control over its own records in what would have amounted to a documents warehouse. A superintendent would have been in nominal charge. Whether or not historical documents would have been housed in the "Hall of Records" is not clear. Probably proponents would have accepted this adjunct in order to broaden the base of support.

The "Hall of Records" question was one of many awaiting answers when Jameson came to Washington to head the Department of Historical Research of the Carnegie Institution of Washington. His interest in it, or the National Archives, as we now know it, was but one of the many projects and activities that claimed time and attention in his busy, purposeful professional life. Characteristically he saw the clear need for it, assessed the situation, and set about achieving what was possible. At first he would have been content to see a hall of records established, assuming that it could and would mature into a true archival institution.

In 1905, hardly a handful of people raised any objections. Ainsworth R. Spofford, who had been appointed Librarian of Congress by Abraham Lincoln, was reported to have wanted the Hall of Records attached in some fashion to the Library.[4] On different occasions it was suggested that the archives building be located on Capitol Hill near the Library and that the archivist be at least nominally responsible to the Librarian. Jameson was quick to point out to all, including the Librarian of Congress, Herbert Putnam, that while such an arrangement might then be suitable, future Librarians would not necessarily be good archivists nor good superintendents of the archival establishment.[5] There was really little need to explain this to Dr. Putnam for he naturally understood the distinction between manuscripts or personal papers and the "main masses of administrative papers."[6]

Many favored a hall of records building, but no one nor even several of them could hope to speak with sufficiently authoritative voice to secure approval of Congress for the erection of the building. Jameson therefore took the matter to the President as he could speak for all the executive agencies.[7] It is of great interest to see Theodore Roosevelt, Jameson and others act within the frame of that trait of the American character which erects a great building, and then creates the agency and appoints the officers who are to preside over it. President Roosevelt thought erecting a hall of records building a "hardly large enough matter to have the thing done."[8] In December, 1907, the President, following Jameson's suggestion, issued an executive order calling for estimates from department heads as to their space requirements. On this occasion Putnam gave his support to the archive movement but made it clear that its functions should not be added to those of the Library of Congress.[9]

The Jameson program of education was underway in the spring of 1908: this was done through conversations with chief clerks, cabinet members, members of Congress, historians and any who would listen. To further this educational program a committee of The American Historical Association was formed on November 27, 1908. Jameson was made its chairman with John B. McMaster and Alfred T. Mahan as members.[10] The chairmanship of the committee thus gave Jameson a logical and valid reason to enquire further into matters that, narrowly interpreted, might have been considered not his business at all.

After William Howard Taft came into office, Jameson urged the President to include a recommendation for an archives building in one of his messages.[11] He further emphasized the pecuniary losses the government must suffer in the destruction of records as those of the Treasury Department without such a safeguard as an archival building. Charles D. Norton, writing for the President, asked if the Library of Congress might be an effective organization through which "to classify, index and store these valuable records?" Jameson in his reply demonstrated the need for a separate building and eventually a distinct agency. The best means of success, judging from the experience of other countries, was to use "the thin edge of the wedge, by providing at first simply a proper archive *building* into which departments might turn all papers which they were content to regard as not needed in their own buildings, and in which such papers might be held as deposits, subject to regulations framed by the department, with respect to storage and accessibility to officials and the public."

The American Historical Association adopted a resolution on December 30, 1910, which was presented to each house of Congress early in 1911.[12] Influencing public opinion was all Jameson and his associates could hope for, and the memorial "will have to be reintroduced next December and followed up the rest of my life or until the building is agreed upon."[13]

Much energy and thought went into discussion of the size, shape and location of the building-to-be. The movement gained strength when President Taft made a forceful recommendation to Congress on February 2, 1912. The Public Buildings Act of March 4, 1913, authorized construction of an archives building, but funds were not appropriated. An Act of August 1, 1914, provided $5,000 to prepare preliminary plans and drawings for the authorized building.

While the gathering of data and the preparation of plans proceeded slowly, Jameson encouraged and directed a steady stream of propaganda in favor of the archives building; this was greatly helped and influenced by the article "The National Archives; A Programme," by Waldo G. Leland.[14]

The war in Europe and America's participation in it together with postwar readjustments effectively shelved plans for the national archives building. Ironically, it was not until the Public Buildings Commission decided in 1926 to fill the Federal Triangle that construction of an archives building was assured. The significant fact is that Jameson had established solidly the need for an archives building in the minds of effective members of Congress.

"Yes, I think we can now be sure," Jameson wrote to Eben Putnam on June 4, 1926, "that the National Archives Building will be erected, and as soon as the slow operations of government building permit. . . . After one of the recent meetings of that (Public Buildings) Commission, the chairman, Senator (Reed) Smoot, announced that the Archives Building would be the first to be taken up, and I gather that he is determined upon this and that there would be no effective opposition. . . ."

A few days later Jameson wrote to a former student, Senator Simeon D. Fess of Ohio, confiding his concern about the creation of an organization to function in the building.[15]

> The objects for which we have sought such a building — security, suitable care, orderly arrangement, ease in laying hands quickly on what is needed for government use or by students,

facility in using and good results from use—can not be secured by a building alone. There must be a high-grade organization, with expert personnel taken over from the contributing departments or secured by special search, and all necessary legislation toward this end ought to be put through in the next session of Congress, because a portion of the staff should be at work, well before the completion of the building, in doing all that can be done beforehand to facilitate the transfer. If the organization of the archive service should wait till the building is ready, the service would be swamped in the beginning, and chaos produced, by the tumbling in of tons of records and papers which departments are in a hurry to get rid of.

But wait the organization did until the Act of June 19, 1934, became law. By that late date all thought of placing the national archives under the general supervision of the Librarian of Congress was forgotten and also forgotten was the "Hall of Records" or warehousing of records idea. A true national archives came into being, and the infant agency was entrusted to a devoted group of men and women under the direction of Archivists of the United States, R. D. W. Connor, Solon J. Buck and Wayne C. Grover. The essential condition of non-partisan, non-political and professional service has been accepted by Congress and five successive Presidents.

It is neither necessary nor appropriate in this brief space to give in tedious detail all the steps Jameson took or avoided in the plans and construction of the building or in the preparation and passage of the establishing act. However tiresome or repetitious or troublesome, each step that was necessary Jameson took and each step that was ill-advised he avoided.

His plan for a commission on historical publications was incorporated in the National Archives establishment. Moribund for more than a decade, the National Historical Publications Commission was revitalized by President Harry S.

Truman in 1950. The Commission has since then under the distinguished leadership of Philip M. Hamer and Oliver W. Holmes fulfilled the ideals and standards for which Jameson hoped.

Quite suitably there is now in the National Archives lobby on the ground floor facing Pennsylvania Avenue a bronze plaque attesting to Jameson's successful efforts in its behalf. But an even greater tribute is the indispensable institution itself to whose creation he devoted much time over so many years.

NOTES

[1] The J. Franklin Jameson Papers in the Library of Congress are the best single source of information for his interest in the creation of the National Archives. Most of the pertinent details from this and other sources are found in the article by Fred Shelley entitled, "The Interest of J. Franklin Jameson in the National Archives: 1908-1934," *The American Archivist* (April, 1949), 99-130.

[2] 55th Congress, 2nd Session, House Document No. 226, and Act of March 3, 1903, Public Law 156.

[3] Root to Jameson, May 26, 1911, Jameson Papers.

[4] Lothrop Withington to Editor, *The Nation*, February 2, 1911, printed in issue of February 16.

[5] A lucid example is found in Jameson to Charles D. Norton, Taft's secretary, November 21, 1910, Jameson Papers.

[6] Putnam to Theodore Roosevelt, December 20, 1907, Jameson Papers.

[7] Jameson to Roosevelt, December 12, 1907, Jameson Papers.

[8] Jameson to Putnam, December 24, 1907, Jameson Papers.

[9] Putnam to Roosevelt, December 20, 1907, Jameson Papers.

[10] Jameson to Henry B. Gardner, January 22, 1919, Jameson Papers.

[11] Jameson to Norton, September 7, November 21, 1910, and Norton to Jameson, September 12 and November 9, 1910, Jameson Papers.

[12] Jameson to Mahan, March 2, 1911, Jameson Papers.

[13] Jameson to Charles Moore, May 13, 1911, Jameson Papers.

[14] *American Historical Review*, October, 1912, Pp. 1-28.

[15] June 23, 1926, Jameson Papers.

JAMESON AS EDITOR

by Boyd C. Shafer

Dr. John Franklin Jameson was our foremost historical editor and still heads our ever lengthening list of scholarly editors. Perhaps this statement needs justification. For me this justification is based on both a study of primary sources and on similar personal experience for later I, too, was the editor of *The American Historical Review*. Here then I shall try to describe and estimate Jameson's contribution as an editor.

In the belief with Croce and Collingwood that history should or must be written, I can thoroughly understand the thorny problems Jameson faced and the excellence he achieved.[1]

The 1880's witnessed a marvelous flowering of academic scholarship throughout the western world. It was in this period that Jameson went to Johns Hopkins where in 1882 he received its first doctorate in American history. This flowering further produced a rich harvest of twentieth century historical scholarship of which Jameson both in his person and activities became a strong and ever continuing influence.

Jameson began thinking of founding an American historical journal in these 1880's, especially after a talk with Dr. Mandell Creighton, Editor of the *English Historical Review*. Years later at a meeting in New York on April 6,

1895, a group of twenty-six historians, of whom Jameson was one, founded *The American Historical Review.* The new Board of Editors[2] chose Jameson, then a professor at Brown University, to be managing editor of the *Review,* which was to be a review (not a journal) of about 800 pages modeled on the *English Historical Review.* Jameson was pleased. He wrote his father:[3]

> The family will be glad to know that the committee on the new "American Historical Review," . . . have [sic] elected me managing editor for one term. To be its first editor is a great pleasure to me. Such a position has long been one of my chief ambitions, and now here we are. It is a responsible and difficult job, but I shall do my best.

Professor William M. Sloane, for the Board of Editors, set down the objectives of the *Review* in the first article, "History and Democracy":[4] (1) there was "no check on the course of historical study in the United States," (2) "no decrease in the number of historical writers," and (3) "the reading public was daily enlarging." These aspects of American life created a grave responsibility for "co-ordination and intelligent criticism in historical work." A group of disinterested men accepted this responsibility. Their new *Review* would "display the largest catholicity possible and an impartiality willing always to hear the other side," and would "in no sense be an organ of any school, locality, or clique." "Its primary object" was indicated "by its name of *Review,*" though it would "print articles embodying the results of investigation and monographs of importance." It would be "fearless to denounce a bad or superficial book . . . equally courageous to sustain one which presents unpopular truth." It would, in addition, "assist historical scholars by furnishing materials that could not otherwise be published, and by keeping its professional readers abreast with the latest news in the field . . . ."[5]

Early in their deliberations the editors also formulated their standards for articles and reviews. For articles their three criteria were: "that they shall be fresh and original in treatment; that they shall be the result of accurate scholarship; and that they shall have distinct literary merit." For reviews the editors desired that,[6]

> the review of a book shall be such as will convey to the reader a clear and comprehensive notion of its nature, of its contents, of its merits, of its place in the literature of the subject, and of the amount of its positive contribution to knowledge. .... It is hoped that the reviewer will take pains, first of all, to apprehend the author's conception of the nature and intent of his book and to criticize it with a due regard to its species and purpose. It should, however, be remembered that the review is intended for the information and assistance of readers, and not for the satisfaction of the author of the book. Sympathy, courtesy, a sense of attachment, readiness to make allowance for a different point of view, should not therefore withhold the reviewer from the straightforward expression of adverse judgment sincerely entertained; otherwise the Review cannot fulfill the important function of upholding a high standard of historical writing.

From the beginning the editors resolved that they would never "favor any particular school or . . . sustain any doctrinal tendency in American historical work." They wished "their journal to be the organ of no circle less extensive than the whole American historical profession," and hence had no "policy," but "while maintaining high standards of method and of scholarship to be catholic in matters of opinion."[7]

The full story of the early days and difficulties of the *Review* is yet to be told. Jameson edited the first number,[8] that of October 1895, and continued to edit it for six years through the volumes for 1895-1901, and again for twenty-three years from 1905 to 1928. The *Review* thus became his as well as that of all American historians.

The first Board of Editors included several of the most distinguished historians of the day. The members both

supervised and assisted the Managing Editor. But from the
first Jameson's was the deciding voice. He ultimately determined how policies (which he had a hand in establishing)
would be carried out; he did the editing; he coped with "the
quarterly crisis of the *Review* [*sic*]." He edited copy. He
suggested and solicited articles. He obtained, often with
great difficulty at the beginning, books for review, selected
reviewers, determined the length of reviews, and corre-
sponded with those reviewers who wanted more space or
had other problems. He obtained and selected materials for
the documents section and meticulously edited them. He
wrote accounts of the meetings of the Association and of its
committees. And during the first years he himself wrote
the "notes and news" sections. Later, as he built a staff at
the Carnegie Institution, he was able to turn over some
tasks to assistants, but always it was he who made the major
decisions. Seldom did his editorial vigilance relax: few indeed were the typographical or factual slips during his
twenty-nine years.

Thus in due time Jameson acquired that most enviable
position, an historian's historian. He upheld the highest
historical standards in articles, reviews, and editing of documents. He accepted articles graciously and then somehow
made them better. He rejected articles, usually politely,
occasionally abruptly. Sometimes he gave suggestions to
authors which enabled them to publish elsewhere. Often
he suggested topics for articles and then helped the authors
until these became publishable. But though the *Review* was
"edited primarily in the interest of its readers," never did
he print "an article in order to please a friend." In fact,
he himself set standards for historical editing in America.

This editing was not limited to the *Review*. For example,
he edited the letters of Phineas Bond, John C. Calhoun, and
Stephen Higginson, and the *Original Narratives of Early
American History*. His masterly reply to a confused critic
of his editing of Calhoun's *Correspondence* illustrates a major tenet of all his editing.[9]

> Dealing with a time so subject to controversy,
> and making inevitably a selection from among
> papers too numerous for total publication, I con-
> sidered it no small advantage to be able to say
> ... that no omissions had "been made for ulterior
> purpose—patriotism or partiality, hero worship
> or conventional decorum .... No passages have
> been omitted in order to support or to weaken
> any particular opinions in politics of history.
> Nor has a single word been omitted for the
> supposed benefit of Calhoun's reputation."

An editor who waits on others to present him with materials
to edit is doing only part of his job. It is not an exaggeration
to say that Jameson's imaginative suggestions were behind
most of the serious historical editing done in the United
States from 1890.

As editor of *The American Historical Review*, as head of
the Bureau of Historical Research of the Carnegie Institution, or as Chairman of the Manuscripts Commission of
The American Historical Association, he suggested the
guides to American materials in European archives, the
Records of the Federal Convention, the *Atlas of Historical
Geography*, and the *Dictionary of American Biography*, and
dozens of other volumes. He was the "father" of the National
Archives and of the National Historical Publications Commission which has fostered the publication of papers of
famous Americans and other important documents. He
sponsored and provided for the *Writings in American History*, and the *List of Doctoral Dissertations*. Not only was
he the instigator of these and other editing and archival
projects, but he often had a hand in the actual work done,
sometimes anonymously editing, always counseling, somehow always setting the standards. The character of this
"hand behind" is best revealed in his correspondence with
the late Senator Beveridge when the latter was writing his
Marshall and his *Lincoln*.[10]

As Ranke set standards for the *Historische Zeitschrift*
and for German historians, and Gabriel Monod for the

Revue Historique and French historians, Jameson set standards for *The American Historical Review* and historians of
the United States. He was the wise counselor of American
historians in their wars against ignorance of the past.
Jameson thought his work inferior to that of "learned historians." He "could never be," he wrote in 1903, "an excellent historian," and he was not, as he knew, "a first-rate
teacher"; his talent, "if any," was in "the direction of
Heuristik." As late as 1924 he wrote to his friend Haskins,
"I should like to have written learned books myself . . . ."[11]
His talent was "heuristik"; he was, as he liked to say, a
maker of "bricks for others to use." He was more! It is not
usual to say, as he well knew, that editors are creative, but
he was.

Perhaps he wrote his own best epitaph in writing about
the *Review* seventeen years before he died:[12]

> If the work of the future is to be such as we could
> neither estimate nor perhaps understand, at least
> we shall have left to it a comprehensive record
> of our doings, and full evidence of what we have
> thought in matters of history. Twenty-five vol-
> umes [seven more under his editorship were to
> come], twenty-two thousand pages of print, two
> or three cubic feet of rather solid historical
> matter! . . . It might have been better; it must
> have been useful.

It was.

NOTES

[1] Jameson's papers are in the Manuscript Division of the Library
of Congress. This essay is based chiefly on Elizabeth Donnan and
Leo F. Stock, eds., *An Historian's World. Selections from the Correspondence of John Franklin Jameson*, Philadelphia, The American
Philosophical Society, 1956; the files of *The American Historical Review*, 1895-1901, 1905-1928; the *Annual Reports* of the Association for
the same dates; miscellaneous files in the office of the American Historical Association; conversations with Miss Patty Washington, Dr.
Waldo Leland, and Dr. Samuel Flagg Bemis; and four articles in
The American Historical Review, William Sloane, "History and Democracy," vol. I, Oct. 1895, Pp. 1-23; J. Franklin Jameson, "The American

Historical Association, 1884-1909," vol. XV, Oct. 1909, Pp. 1-20; J. Franklin Jameson, "*The American Historical Review*, 1885-1920," vol. XXVI, Oct. 1920, Pp. 1-17; and "John Franklin Jameson," vol. XLIII, Jan. 1938, Pp. 243-52.

2 Members of the first Board were: George B. Adams, Albert Bushnell Hart, John Bach McMaster, William M. Sloane, H. Morse Stephens, and Harry Pratt Judson, who was added before the first issue.

3 *An Historian's World*, p. 65.

4 Fritz Stern did not include Sloane's essay in his *The Varieties of History*, New York, Meridian Books, 1956, because, as he once told me, he did not know that it was the prospectus for the new *The American Historical Review*. It was.

5 Sloane, *The American Historical Review*, vol. I, Pp. 21-22. The general format of the *Review* (and of most historical reviews) has remained generally the same as it was in 1895. In the 1940's, the documents section of *The American Historical Review* was eliminated and more bibliographical lists of articles were added. In 1962, some of the news section was transferred to the new Association *Newsletter*.

6 Jameson, *The American Historical Review*, XXVI, Pp. 8 and 13.

7 *Ibid.*, p. 8.

8 In addition to Sloane, the distinguished contributors of articles for the first number were Moses Coit Tyler, Henry C. Lea, Henry Adams, and Frederick Jackson Turner. As Jameson himself noted the contributions of Lea and Adams were slight and Lea's article in the second number was weightier.

9 *An Historian's World*, p. 106.

10 See Elizabeth Donnan and Leo F. Stock, eds., *Mississippi Valley Historical Review*, vol. 35, Dec. 1948, March 1949, Pp. 466-92 and 641-73.

11 *An Historian's World*, Pp. 86, 301.

12 *The American Historical Review*, vol. XXVI, p. 17.

J. F. J.

by David C. Mearns

It is awesome to serve as caretaker of one of the enlivened monuments raised (and rising still) to the memory of Franklin Jameson. Here his spirit is encountered daily. The marks of his wisdom, the graces of his learning, the universality of his interests and concern, the receding horizons of his aspirations, and the slow, patient fulfillment of his beginnings are everywhere around. In the course of the past decade, I have come better to understand the magnitude of his achievement and the forces of his personality than ever I did in the days when the Library felt his physical presence.

This is not to say that I do not clearly remember his erect bearing, his carefully parted hair, his close-cropped beard, his faultless grooming, his pleasant voice, his incorruptible dignity. He was constantly visible: sometimes seated at his desk behind that glass screen in the northwest pavilion, standing in Alcove 2 with a volume of Pauly-Wissowa in his hand, crouching before low shelves in the stacks while checking references, or walking briskly up the marble staircase, his coattails flying.

There was a bright afternoon in March, 1937. I was leaning against the balustrade of the Library's main entrance, when I saw Dr. Jameson step from the curb below, onto the street, and directly in the path of an oncoming car, which felled him. A taxi driver and I lifted him and laid him on the back seat of the cab, and, while I knelt on the floor to prevent him from falling, he was rushed to Casualty Hospital. His pain was intense; his leg had been broken; but his expression was calm, even emotionless.

By August he had recovered sufficiently to go to his summer home at North Edgecomb, Maine. On St. Bartholomew's Day he wrote to Herbert Putnam: "I am still on crutches and am likely to be when I return to the Library." He did not return to the Library, but he did come back to Washington.

A fortnight before his death I went to see him about a matter connected with the commemoration of the sesquicentennial of the Constitutional Convention. Upon reaching his home on Que Street, I was ushered to an upstairs room. Dr. Jameson was sitting bolt upright in bed. He seemed to have grown to a giant's size. I suspect that he is growing still.

JOHN FRANKLIN JAMESON: A BIBLIOGRAPHY

*by Donald H. Mugridge**

The following bibliography is an attempt to list all the published writings of Dr. Jameson and all historical texts edited by him, together with the relatively few items about him which have appeared since his death in 1937. The arrangement is chronological by years, with books or lesser separates put first, and articles in periodicals following according to the month or whatever of issue. No attempt has been made to separate materials written and edited. Most of the memorial or biographical literature has taken the form of publication of his letters or other pieces; the few strictly biographical items by other hands have been placed after the former on the few occasions necessary.

Dr. Jameson's distinction is to have sacrificed his own potentialities as a writer of history in the interest of the organization of historical scholarship in the United States and in the civilized world, and to have put his main effort into facilitating the labors of other historians and raising the general standards of the historical profession. Notwithstanding this just fame, the present list makes it evident that his output over his own signature, or sometimes without it, was substantial—no doubt in large part because he started early, at the age of twenty-three, and continued for well over half a century. Edited items no doubt predominate, but a well-edited text hitherto unpublished or partially missing or garbled may be quite as important a contribution to historical knowledge as an original composition.

Because of the importance of cooperation in Dr. Jameson's scheme of things, it is often difficult to know just where his participation begins or ends, and consequently what to include or exclude here. He was, for instance, in general charge of the whole publication program of the Department of Historical Research of the Carnegie Institution of Washington, and those series that were completed after his death had also been planned and provided for by him. But the several publications, apart from the briefest of introductory notes, were in no sense his individual handiwork, and we have therefore left them to his biography rather than his bibliography. His annual reports, both at the Carnegie and at the Library of Congress (in the abbreviated form in which they appear in the reports of the Librarian), are of course listed.

Listed, however, in the concise or summary form which has been adopted for this bibliography, since it is intended as a record of intellectual achievement rather than a guide for collectors or any other objective leading to a multiplication of bibliographical minutiae. Similarly the first, or the most important publication, is deemed a sufficient entry; thus the book publication of *The History of Historical Writing in America* is made the occasion for a note summarizing its earlier appearances in German and American periodicals.

From this among other titles another conclusion becomes clear: however immersed he may have been in the necessary labor on hand, Dr. Jameson throughout his life thought deeply and critically about the nature and the implications of his discipline. At times he was concerned to relate history-writing to the major intellectual currents of the age in which it was done. At others he was concerned to collect examples from which a striking generalization or perhaps a "law of history" could emerge—a major preoccupation of his contemporaries.

But Dr. Jameson was, in the first generation of professional historical scholarship in the United States, exceptional in the sureness with which he drew toward the full acceptance of what was once known as "the New History" and is now perhaps best described as integral history, with no aspect of human life excluded or regarded as irrelevant. There were at least two sources for this wider vision which drew him from an original concentration on constitutional developments. One was the background of a thorough classical education, such as hardly an American historian of the present day receives, with its many-sided approach to the Graeco-Roman world. Another was a strong personal sense of the importance of religion in the history of the New World as much as of the Old, which made him conscious of the shallowness of any presentation which left it out. And thus his *American Revolution Considered as a Social Movement*—which goes back to lectures delivered in 1895, long before the New History had been heard of—is in fact a study in integral history, tracing the effects of a great social convulsion in one sphere after another.

The entries below are a modification of Library of Congress style, and the Library of Congress call number regularly follows an entry. The American Historical Association and *The American Historical Review* are regularly represented by their initials. The compilation was done under a number of handicaps, and the omissions which will doubtless come to light are apologized for in advance.

* Mr. Mugridge died November 3, 1964, less than a week after he had completed this bibliography of Jameson.

A BIBLIOGRAPHY OF
J. FRANKLIN JAMESON'S WRITING

1882

History of the Class of '79. Amherst College, from their graduation to
their first reunion. Compiled from their letters by the class-secretary,
and printed for the use of the class. 1879-1882. Worcester, Mass.,
F. S. Blanchard & Co., 1882. 23 p.

Jameson: p. 12

The indefatigable class secretary had taken on a job that lasted
as long as his life, in the course of which he produced ten reports
and two supplements, as follows:

History of the class of 1879 in Amherst College, from 1882 to 1889.
Compiled by the secretary of the class, chiefly from letters from its
members, and printed for their use. Boston, A. Mudge, 1889. 21 p.

The title pages of the reports follow this style henceforward,
save that with the 1889-1904 report the comma after "College"
disappears. Therefore we abbreviate.

... from 1889 to 1904. ... Lancaster, Pa., New Era Ptg. Co., 1904.
31 p.

'79 Supplement to Class history, July 1904. n.p. 9 p., 1 1.

... from 1904 to 1909. ... Brunswick, Me., Record Press [1909]. 34 p.

Supplement to the "History ... from 1904 to 1909." n.p. 7 p.

A.C. '79. ... The Goshen quadruplets. n.p. 2 1.
ms. note at end: "And it was all a fake! They were not authentic.
J.F.J."

... from 1909 to 1914. ... Washington, Press of Byron S. Adams
[1914]. 51 p.

'79. Supplement to Class history, July 1914. n.p., n.d. 16 p. p. 10-16.
Hiram's poem [in four-footed anapaestic couplets].

. . . from 1914 to 1919. . . . Washington, C. E. Gouls [1919]. 49 p.

Amherst College, '79. Supplement to Class history, June, 1919. [n.p.,
1919]. [4 p.]

. . . from 1919 to 1924. . . . Washington, Columbian Ptg. Co. [1924].
44 p.

. . . from 1924 to 1929. . . . Washington, Columbian Ptg. Co. [1929].
33 p.

"This is the tenth of these quinquennial pamphlets. . . . Perhaps
it is the last, for printing costs increase as our numbers diminish,
and perhaps at the approaching meeting the class may resolve on
some simpler form of report."

The origin and development of the municipal government of New
York City. I. The Dutch period. II. The English and American
period. *Magazine of American History,* v. 8, May: 315-330; Sept.:
598-611.

1883

Bibliography of Monroe, and the Monroe Doctrine. In Daniel C. Gilman. *James Monroe in his relations to the public service during
half a century, 1776-1826.* Boston, Houghton Mifflin, 1883. P. 253-
280.   E372. G48.

Reissued in 1892.

In the revised edition of 1898, President Gilman's Preface referred
to the great utility of J. F. J.'s bibliography and acknowledged
his obligation. He also stated that it "has been revised and enlarged for this edition," evidently not by J. F. J. (p. 260-294).
As enlarged, it was reprinted in the issues of 1909 and 1911.

"This article contained the substance of the many submitted by
Jameson as part of his work for the 'Ph.D.'" Elizabeth Donnan
and Leo F. Stock (eds.), *An Historian's World, Selections from
the Correspondence of John Franklin Jameson.* Philadelphia, 1956,
p. 25, n. 50.

"The common-land system was brought over from old England
to most of the New England towns; but nowhere has it played a
more important part than in Easthampton, Long Island."

Montauk and the common lands of Easthampton. *Magazine of American History,* v. 9, Apr. 1883: 225-239.   E171. M18, v. 9.

1884

Records of the town of Amherst, from 1735 to 1788. Reprinted from the Amherst Record. Edited by J. F. Jameson. Amherst, Mass., Press of J. E. Williams, 1884. IV, 100 p.

Records of Hadley Third Precinct, 1735-53, of Hadley Second Precinct, 1754-58, and of the District of Amherst, 1759-75; town records begin on Jan. 24, 1776 (p. 69). This self-financing publication was the product of J.'s summer vacation, June 1883: See Donnan and Stock, p. 28, n. 70.

1886

An Introduction to the Study of the Constitutional and Political History of the States. Baltimore: Johns Hopkins Press, May 1886. 29 p. (Johns Hopkins University Studies in historical and political science, 4th series, no. 5.)

Three papers read to the "historical seminary" of Johns Hopkins, January 1885; the first was also read at the meeting of The American Historical Association at Saratoga, September 1885.

1887

William Usselinx [1567-1647], founder of the Dutch and Swedish West India companies. A.H.A., Papers, v. 2, no. 3. New York: Putnam, 1887. p. [149]-382. 234 p.   E172. A65 1887

Bibliography. p. 201-220.

"Abstract" of extracts read at 3rd annual meeting of the A.H.A., Washington, Apr. 29, 1886. Papers, v. 2, no. 1: p. 83-85. These *Papers* have an unusual double pagination, one for the volume and another for the individual item.

1889

The Predecessor of the Supreme Court. Essays in the constitutional history of the United States in the formative period, 1775-1789, by graduates and former members of the Johns Hopkins University, edited by J.F.J. Boston: Houghton Mifflin, 1889. p. 1-45.

xiii, 321 p.   JK 119.J3

Essays on the const. hist. of the U. S., 1775-1789.

Reviews—*Dial,* v. 10, Mar. 1890: 311
   English Historical Review, v. 6, Oct. 1891: 788
   Magazine of American History, v. 23, Feb. 1890: 176
   New Englander, v. 52 (n.s. v. 16), Feb. 1890: 170-171

Overland, 2d Ser., v. 15, Apr. 1890: 442

Political Science Quarterly, v. 5, Dec. 1890: 696-697

The Old Federal Court of Appeal. A.H.A., Papers. New York, 1889. v. 3, no. 2, p. [381]-392.   E172. A60 1889

"Somewhat abridged." Read at the 5th annual meeting of the A.H.A., Washington, Dec. 27, 1888; v. 3, no. 2 is Herbert B. Adams report of its proceedings.

1890

Did the Fathers Vote? *New England Magazine,* n.s. v. 1, Jan. 1890: 484-490.   AP2. N4, n.s., v. 1

Illustrates, from Massachusetts figures of the 1770's and '80's, the small numbers qualified to vote, and the even smaller ones who troubled to do so.

Letters to Herbert B. Adams, Feb. 21 and July 2, 1890. *In Historical Scholarship in the United States, 1876-1901: as revealed in the correspondence of Herbert B. Adams.* Edited by W. Stull Holt. Baltimore: Johns Hopkins Press, 1938. p. 127-129; 134-135.

E175, 5, H1797

Other references to J.F.J. in the letters and in Holt's introduction may be found through the index.

The Development of Modern European Historiography. *Atlantic Monthly,* v. 66, Sept. 1890: 322-333.   AP2. A8, v. 66

From the Renaissance to Ranke and his school.

An Early Briton. *The Chautauquan,* v. 12, Oct. 1890: 24-28

AP2. C48, v. 12

This and next year's contribution were, no doubt, potboilers, but each is done with the greatest care and polish.

1891

The History of Historical Writing in America. Boston: Houghton Mifflin, 1891. 160 p.

Originated as public lectures at Johns Hopkins University in Jan.-Feb. 1887; repeated at Brown University, Feb.-Mar. 1889.

Historical Writing in the United States, 1783-1861.

A public lecture delivered in the hall of the Johns Hopkins University. *Englische Studien* (Heilbonn) 12 Band, 1 Heft (1888): 59-77.

Historical Writing in the United States since 1861.
A public [etc.]. Do., 13 Band, 2 Heft (1889) : 230-246.
                                                    PE3. E6, v. 12, 13.

Probably the text as originally delivered; J.F.J. elected to omit from the later printings his tribute "to the enthusiasm, the versatile energy, the good judgment, and the wise catholicity of my chief in office, Dr. Herbert B. Adams."

History of Historical Writing in America.
New England Magazine, n.s., v. 3, Jan. 1891: 645-655; Feb.: 721-731; v. 4, Mar. 1811: 113-124; Apr.: 250-260
                                                    AP2. N4, n.s., v. 3, 4

Practically identical with the book, although the title of the 4th part is altered and the first sentence dropped in the book.

History of Historical Writing.

Reviewed in *English Historical Review*, v. 8, Jan. 1893: 177-179.
An English Sea-rover. *The Chautauquan*, v. 13, Apr. 1891: 21-25.
                                                    AP2. C48, v. 13.

Drake, Hawkins *et al.*, as reported in Hakluyt's *Voyages*.

The Expenditures of Foreign Governments in Behalf of History.
American Historical Association, *Annual Report*, 1891 (Washington: G.P.O., 1892), 31-61.   E172. A60 1891

A paper read at the 8th annual meeting of the AHA, Washington, Dec. 29-31, 1891. P. 44-61 consist of texts or translations of 19 letters or other communications from foreign officials or American representatives abroad, on which the paper was based. Actually, at the moment, American expenditure in support of history was "relatively greater than any" European country, but solely because of the large cost of the *Official Records of the Rebellion*, and there was no provision for continuing work.

Lowell and Public Affairs. *Review of Reviews*, v. 4, Oct. 1891: 287-291.
                                                    AP2. R4, v. 4

First part of "James Russell Lowell: a composite character sketch," with 4 other contributors (p. 286-310).

1892

Two Virginians. *Atlantic Monthly*, v. 70, Sept. 1892: 407-414.
                                                    AP2. A8, v. 70

Unsigned review of William Wirt Henry's *Patrick Henry* (New York: Scribner, 1891. 3 v.) and Kate Mason Rowland's *The Life*

of George Mason (New York: Putnam, 1892. 2 v.). Referred to in
J.F.J.'s letter to Sarah Elwell (later Mrs. J.), July 4, 1892 (Donnan
and Stock, p. 61).

1893

Greek History and the Constitution of the United States.
The Chautauquan, v. 17, June 1893: 285-289.

                                                      AP2. C48, v. 17

In the writings of John Adams, Monroe, and in the *Federalist,*
especially no. 18. The subject has received very little attention since.

Virginia Voting in the Colonial Period (1744-1774). *Nation,* v. 56,
Apr. 27, 1893: 309-310.

                                                      AP2. N3, v. 56

Figures in 13 cases indicate that about 6% of the white population
voted—a larger proportion than in other parts of America a little
later.

1894

Dictionary of United States History, 1492-1894. Four centuries of
history. Written concisely and arranged alphabetically in dictionary
form. Boston: Puritan Pub. Co. (1894), 733 p.

Copyright James Drummond Ball   E174. J31

Reissued in 1895, 1897, 1898.

Same text and pagination issued by History Pub. Co. of Boston,
1898, 1899, and 1900.

Phil.: Historical Pub. Co., c. 1908. 844 p.

Encyclopedic Dictionary of American History by J.F.J. and J.W. Buel
[Wash., D. C., American History Society, 1900], 2 v. (Library of
American History [v. 5-6]).

Jas. Wm. Buel, 1849-1920.

McKinley revised ed., 1901 *Encyclopedic Dictionary of American
Reference.*

Buel omitted a percentage of the articles, replacing them with a
smaller number on such timely subjects as Aguinaldo, the Alaskan
gold rush, etc.

The Library of American History brought in J. C. Redpath and
M. J. Wright.

"The Analytical Reference,"—v. 1—Dict. [J.W.B.], v. 2 [Addenda],
v. 4, Columbus [another book job of Buel's], 5, 6, Redpath, "in an
attached and continuous story."

Encyclopedic Dictionary. Editorial board Gen. Marcus J. Wright . . .
Prof. J. Franklin Jameson. . . . J. W. Buel [at bottom], Wash.,
National University Society [1904].

V. 3 is a Supplement, containing the matter omitted from the
1894 ed. Additions, chiefly biographical.
[c. 1906]   1909 card

Dictionary of United States History; alphabetical, chronological,
statistical, from the earliest explorations to the present time; based
upon the original work prepared in 1893 by J. Franklin Jameson.
Rev. ed., edited under the supervision of Albert E. McKinley . . .
Philadelphia: Historical Publishing Co., 1931. 874 p.

E174. J319

The Origin of the Standing Committee System in American Legislative
Bodies. *Political Science Quarterly,* v. 9, June 1894: 246-267.

JA1. P76

Also AHA, *Annual Report* for 1893, p. 393-399.

E172. A60 1893

Also papers from the historical seminar of Brown University.

Papers from the Historical Seminar of Brown University, edited by
J. Franklin Jameson. Nos. 1-10. Providence, R. I., 1894-1899.

All except no. 6, Gertrude Selwyn Kimball's "The East India
Trade of Providence from 1787 to 1807," are separate printings
from other serials. Separate paginations, the two from the *Annual
Reports* of the AHA having the numbers which occur in those vol-
umes. No. 4 is JFJ's "The Origin of the Standing Committee System
in American Legislative Bodies," reprinted from the *Political
Science Quarterly,* June 1894, and also with the original pagination.
The authors may be listed as a roll of J.F.J.'s pupils during his decade at Brown: Neil Andrews, Mary E. Wooley [President of Mount
Holyoke College, 1900-1937]; Charles Stickney; William D. John-
ston; Gertrude Selwyn Kimball; Harold D. Hazeltine [Downing
Professor of the Laws of England, Cambridge U., 1919-1942]; Marcus W. Jernegan; Edmund C. Burnett; and Louis Hamilton Meades.

1895

The American Historical Review. Managing editor, J. Franklin Jameson. V. 1, no. 1, Oct. 1895—v. 6, no. 4, July 1901. V. 11, no. 1, Oct.
1905—v. 33, no. 4, July 1928. (The editor of v. 7-10 was Andrew C.
McLaughlin.)

[Unsigned review of John Brown, *The Pilgrim Fathers of New England and their Puritan Successors* (New York: F. H. Powell, 1895),
v. 1, Apr. 1896: 541-542.]

1896

Diary of Edward Hooker, 1805-1808. [Edited by] J. Franklin Jameson. AHA, *Annual Report for 1896* (Washington, 1897), p. 842-929.

EN. A60 1896

Hooker (1785-1846) was a descendant of Thomas Hooker and a Yale graduate who, during these years, was teaching and studying law in Columbia, S. C. J.F.J.'s selections are largely confined to matters of political rather than social interest.

[Bibliography of] Procedings, etc., of Early Party Conventions [1795, 1808-32]. *AHR*, v. 1, July 1896: 760-771.

E171. A57, v. 1

Symbols indicate the holdings of 15 libraries.

1897 [6?]

Report on Spanish and Dutch settlements prior to 1648. In U. S. *Commission to Investigate and Report upon the True Divisional Line between the Republic of Venezuela and British Guiana*. Report and accompanying papers. (Washington: G.P.O., 1896-97.) v. 1.

F2331. B72 US, v. 1

1897

Letters of Stephen Higginson, 1783-1804. Edited by J.F.J. (Washington: G.P.O., 1897), p. 704-841.

E301. H63

"From the Report of the Historical Manuscripts Commission of the American Historical Association for 1896."

57 letters, a majority of them to Timothy Pickering.

John Lothrop Motley (1814-1877). *In Library of the World's best literature, ancient and modern*. Charles Dudley Warner, editor. New York: R. S. Peale and J. S. Hill. V. 18: 10373-10380.

PN6013. W27, v. 18

A biographical sketch, with J.F.J.'s signature in facsimile, prefacing 25 pages of extracts from three of Motley's histories. The set was several times reissued, without material change.

The Functions of State and Local Historical Societies with Respect to Research and Publication. American Historical Association. *Annual Report for 1897* (Washington: G.P.O., 1898), p. 51-59.

Contributed to a discussion of the functions of local historical societies, Cleveland, Dec. 30, 1897; R. G. Thwaites and J. F. Wright (Oberlin) were the other speakers.

The Colonial Assemblies and Their Legislative Journals. [Compiled by] J. Franklin Jameson. AHA, *Annual Report for 1897* (Washington, 1898), p. 403-453.

E172. A60 1897

Lists of journals of 12 colonies, especially those which were then unpublished or only partially published. Goes to 1800 in some cases, and includes four Canadian Provinces and Tennessee as well as some of the Old Thirteen.

President Andrews and the Situation at Brown. American monthly *Review of Reviews*, v. 16, Sept. 1897: 310-316.

Published anonymously.

The Early Political Uses of the Word Convention. American Antiquarian Society. *Proceedings*, n.s., v. 12, Oct. 1897: 183-196. Worcester, Mass., 1899.

E172. A35, n.s., v. 12

1896-97

Letters of Phineas Bond, British Consul at Philadelphia, to the Foreign Office of Great Britain, 1787-1794. [Edited by] J. Franklin Jameson. AHA, *Annual Report for 1896* (Washington, 1897), p. 513-659; *Annual Report for 1897* (Washington, 1898), p. 454-568.

E172. A60 1896, 1897

102 letters from the Public Record Office, London, of which the first 61, to the end of 1789, are in the *Annual Report for 1896*.

1896-99

Reports of the Historical Manuscripts Commission of the American Historical Association, J.F.J., chairman. Nos. 1-4, 1896-1899 in AHA Annual Reports for 1896-99, as follows:

E172. A60

1. *Annual Report for 1896* (Washington: G.P.O., 1897), p. 463-1107. Report proper, p. 467-480; 3 of the 6 following parts were edited by J.F.J. (see above) and a fourth, "A List of Printed Guides to and Descriptions of Archives and Other Repositories of Historical Manuscript," was prepared by Edmund C. Burnett under his direction.

2. *Annual Report for 1897* (Washington: G.P.O., 1898), p. 397-679. Report proper, p. 399-403. 2 of the 3 following parts were edited by J.F.J.

3. *Annual Report for 1898* (Washington: G.P.O., 1899), p. 565-708. Report proper, p. 567-572, indicating that the effort was going

into the Calhoun correspondence. The three appendices were compiled by Edmund C. Burnett, John Pettibone, and Gertrude S. Kimball, all under J.F.J.'s direction.

4. *Annual Report for 1899*, v. 2.

With the Calhoun correspondence, the Commission suspended its labors, exhausting chiefly to J.F.J., who resigned as chairman. In 1906 he was induced to resume the chairmanship, but let himself be drawn into no such a treadmill. (The only considerable contributor, besides J.F.J. and his pupils, had been Frederick J. Turner.) He remained chairman through 1908, when he was able to unload the job onto Worthington C. Ford. *Diplomatic Correspondence of the Republic of Texas*, edited by George P. Garrison, published in 3 volumes, 1 of which was a part of the *Annual Report for 1907*, and the other 2 of the *Report for 1908*, was formally the 8th Report of the Historical Manuscripts Commission, with a letter of transmittal, the first signature on which was J.F.J.'s. (*Report for 1907*, v. 2: p. 5.)

1898

The Early Political Uses of the Word Convention. *AHR*, v. 3, Apr. 1898: 477-487.

E171. A57, v. 3

Also in American Antiquarian Society.

1899

Correspondence of John C. Calhoun. Edited by J. Franklin Jameson. AHA, *Annual Report for 1899*, v. 2 (Washington: G.P.O., 1900), 1218 p.

E172. A60, v. 2 1899

Constituted the 4th annual report of the Historical Manuscripts Commission. Includes letters of Calhoun, 1804-1850 (p. 93-785), letters to Calhoun, 1827-1850 (p. 791-1212), and a Calendar of Calhoun's letters heretofore printed (p. 25-46). The letters are preceded by an Account of Calhoun's early life by William Pinkney Starke, transcribed from the shorthand of the manuscript and "compressed" by J.F.J. (p. 65-89). There are also a preface, a Calhoun chronology, and an index. The immense volume is perhaps Dr. Jameson's most impressive work of scholarship, particularly so when one considers the other things he had on hand at the time.

1900

Letters of Ebenezer Huntington, 1774-1781 [edited by J.F.J.]. *AHR*, v. 5, July 1900: 702-729.

E171. A57, v. 5

32 family letters from an officer in the Continental Army.

Diary of John Harrower, 1773-1776 [edited by J.F.J.]. *AHR*, v. 6, Oct. 1900: 65-107.

E171. A57, v. 6

Diary of a Scottish indentured servant in Virginia.

1901

Chicago, Nov. 23

[J.F.J.] To the Members of the Executive Council of the American Historical Association. Signed, J. F. Jameson, re-establishing a School of Amer. Historical Studies at Washington, with Dr. Herbert Adams' bequest of $5,000 as a nucleus.

printed   Box 5 file 60   folder, 2 1.

Letters on the Nullification Movement in South Carolina, 1830-1834 [edited by J.F.J.]. *AHR*, v. 6, July 1901: 736-765; v. 7, Oct. 1901: 92-119.

E171. A57, v. 6, 7

57 letters, mostly from the papers of James H. Hammond and Francis W. Pickens.

Letter of John Quincy Adams, 1811 [edited by J.F.J.]. *AHR*, v. 6, Jan. 1901: 341-344.

E171. A57, v. 6

A letter addressed to the Secretary of State (James Monroe).

Letters of Dr. Thomas Cooper, 1825-1832 [edited by J.F.J.]. *AHR*, v. 6, July 1901: 725-736.

E171. A57, v. 6

Correspondence relating to his ". . . petition for the restoration of the fine inflicted upon him by Justice Chase. . . ."

1902

Studies in the history of the Federal Convention of 1787. AHA, *Annual Report for 1902*. Washington: G.P.O., 1903. v. 1: 87-167.

E172. A60 1902

"Of the [10] papers here printed, the first ["Letters from the Federal Convention"] was read at the Philadelphia meeting of the

Association [Dec. 27, 1902]. The rest owe their presence here to the merciful institution known as 'leave to print.' The importance of these studies is suggested by the fact that Max Farrand dedicates his authoritative edition of *The Records of the Federal Convention* (New Haven: Yale University Press, 1911) to J.F.J."

JK141. U58

Contents—1. Letters from the Federal Convention.—2. [5] Letters not heretofore printed.—3. List of [86] letters in print.—4. The text of the Virginia Plan.—5. The text of the Pinckney Plan. —6. The text of the New Jersey Plan.—7. The text of Hamilton's plan.—8. The Wilson drafts for the Committee of detail.—9. Members who did not sign.—10. The action of the States.—11. Journal and debates of the State conventions.

Review of Correspondence of John C. Calhoun by Edward Gaylord Bourne. *AHR*, v. 7, Jan. 1902: 372-375.

E171. A57, v. 7

The Influence of Universities upon Historical Writing. *The University Record of the University of Chicago*, v. 6, Jan. 1902: 294-300.

LD908. A2, v. 6

Convention Address delivered Dec. 17, 1901. Introduction of the speaker by Prof. Frederick J. Turner, p. 293-294.

Benefits and dangers of the present age, "in which the leading influence upon historical writing is that of the university and the university professor."

The Johns Hopkins anniversary. *The Dial*, v. 32, Mar. 1, 1902: 143-146.

AP2. D48, v. 32

Exercises and significance of the 25th anniversary of the founding, celebrated on Feb. 21 and 22, 1902.

Review of *The Writings of James Madison*, edited by Gaillard Hunt. Vols. 1 and 2 (New York: Putnam, 1900-01). *AHR*, v. 7, Apr. 1902: 573-575.

E171. A57, v. 7.

Review of Edward Gaylord Bourne's *Essays in Historical Criticism* (New York: Scribner, 1901). *AHR*, v. 7, July 1902: 745-747.

E171. A57, v. 7.

Review of *The Writings of James Monroe*, edited by Stanislaus Murray Hamilton, vol. 5 (New York: Putnam, 1901). *Ibid.*, 781-783.

A letter of Alexander H. Stephens [June 15] 1854. *AHR*, v. 8, Oct. 1902: 91-97.

E171. A57, v. 8

To Robert Sims Burch of Marietta, Ga., a sometime law partner of Stephens; the ms. was then in the possession of Martha Reid Robinson of Chicago.

1903

Review of the Naval Miscellany, edited by John Knox Laughton, vol. 1 (London: Navy Records Society, 1902). *AHR*, v. 8, Apr. 1903: 532-534.

E171. A57, v. 8

Review of *The Writings of James Madison*, edited by Gaillard Hunt, v. 3 (New York: Putnam, 1902). *Ibid.*, 559-561.

E171. A57, v. 8

Portions of Charles Pinckney's Plan for a Constitution, 1787. *AHR*, v. 8, Apr. 1903: 509-511.

E171. A57, v. 8

Advance publication of a document in the handwriting of James Wilson owned by the Historical Society of Pennsylvania.

St. Eustatius in the American Revolution. *AHR*, v. 8, July 1903: 683-708.

E171. A57, v. 8

Review of *The Writings of James Monroe*, edited by Stanislaus Murray Hamilton, vol. 6 (New York: Putnam, 1902). *AHR*, v. 8, July 1903: 781-782.

E171. A57, v. 8

1904

Review of *The Cambridge Modern History*, v. 7, The United States (New York: Macmillan, 1903). *AHR*, v. 9, Jan. 1904: 365-369.

E171. A57, v. 9

Review of *The Writings of James Monroe*, edited by Stanislaus Murray Hamilton, v. 7 (New York: Putnam, 1903) and *The Writings of James Madison*, edited by Gaillard Hunt, v. 4 (New York: Putnam, 1903). *Ibid.*, Apr. 1904: 577-579.

E171. A57, v. 9

A Protest. *Nation*, v. 78, Mar. 17, 1904: 210.

AP2. N2

Letter to the editor on the claims of *The History of North America*, edited by Guy Carleton Lee and Francis Newton Thorpe (Philadelphia, printed for subscribers only by G. Barrie, c. 1903-c. 1907. 20 v.) to have been based on a plan suggested by the AHA. Reprinted in Donnan and Stock, p. 88-89.

1905

Notice of *The Writings of James Madison,* edited by Gaillard Hunt,
v. 5 (New York: Putnam, 1904). *AHR,* v. 10, Apr. 1905: 691-692.

A171. A57, v. 10

1906

Gaps in the Published Records of United States History. *AHR,* v. 11,
July 1906: 817-831.

A paper read before the Columbia Historical Society of Washington, D. C.

Papers of Dr. James McHenry on the Federal Convention of 1787
[edited by J.F.J.]. *AHR,* v. 11, Apr. 1906: 595-624.

E171. A57, v. 11

Papers of a Revolutionary soldier, later Secretary of War.

Letters of Jefferson to Marbois, 1781, 1783 [edited by J.F.J.]. *AHR,*
v. 12, Oct. 1906: 75-77.

E171. A57, v. 12

Two letters to the secretary of the French Legation in the United
States.

Journal of John Muir, 1791 [edited by J.F.J]. *AHR,* v. 12, Oct. 1906:
77-94.

E171. A57, v. 12

Inveterate traveler.

Project of Latin-American Confederation, 1856 [edited by J.F.J.].
AHR, v. 12, Oct. 1906: 94-103.

E171. A57, v. 12

Letter of Stephen R. Mallory, 1861 [edited by J.F.J.]. *AHR,* v. 12,
Oct. 1906: 103-109.

E171. A57, v. 12

Letter from the Confederate Secretary of the Navy to a friend.

Letter of Grant to his Father, on the Capture of Vicksburg, 1863
[edited by J.F.J.]. *AHR,* v. 12, Oct. 1906: 109.

E171. A57, v. 12

1906-17

Original Narratives of Early American History, reproduced under
the auspices of The American Historical Association; general editor,
J. Franklin Jameson. New York: Scribner, 1906-17. 19 v.

E187.07 (A-W)

For the volumes edited individually by J.F.J., see 1909, 1910,
and 1913.

1906-28

Carnegie Institution of Washington. Department of Historical Research. *Annual Report of the Director, J. Franklin Jameson.* 1906-1919. Washington, D. C., 1907-1920. 14 v. in 1.

E172. C28

Extracted from the Year Books of the Carnegie Institution, v. 5-18.

——————— ——————— 1919-1928. Washington, D. C., 1920-1928. 8 v. in 1.

E172. C28

Should be 9; extract from Year Book 24 missing.

1907

Letters of Thomas Newe from South Carolina, 1682 [edited by J.F.J.]. *AHR*, v. 12, Jan. 1907: 322-327.

E171. A57, v. 12

Three letters to his father.

Narrative of a Voyage to Maryland, 1705-1706 [edited by J.F.J.]. *AHR*, v. 12, Jan. 1907: 327-340.

E171. A57, v. 12

Author unknown.

Intercepted Letters of Virginian Tories, 1775 [edited by J.F.J.] *AHR*, v. 12, Jan. 1907: 341-346.

E171. A57, v. 12

Letter of John Marshall to James Wilkinson, 1787 [edited by J.F.J.]. *AHR*, v. 12, Jan. 1907: 346-348.

E171. A57, v. 12

Letter to Gen. James Wilkinson, U.S.A.

Gilman v. *McClary:* A New Hampshire Case of 1791 [edited by J.F.J.]. *AHR*, v. 12, Jan. 1907: 348-350.

E171. A57, v. 12

A case in which a legislative act was declared unconstitutional.

The Catholic Mission in Maryland, 1641 [edited by J.F.J.]. *AHR*, v. 12, Apr. 1907: 584-587.

E171. A57, v. 12

Edmund Randolph on the British Treaty, 1795 [edited by J.F.J.]. *AHR*, v. 12, Apr. 1907: 587-599.

E171. A57, v. 12

Virgil Maxcy on Calhoun's Political Opinions and Prospects, 1823 [edited by J.F.J.]. *AHR*, v. 12, Apr. 1907: 599-601.

E171. A57, v. 12

Maxcy, a prominent politician and lawyer and an ardent supporter of Calhoun.

1908

The American Acta Sanctorum. *AHR*, v. 13, Jan. 1908: 286-302.

E171. A57, v. 13

J.F.J.'s address as President of the AHA, delivered at Madison, Wisconsin, Dec. 27, 1907.

1909

Narratives of New Netherland, 1609-1664; edited by J. Franklin Jameson. New York: Scribner, 1909. xx, 478 p.

F122. 1.J31

The American Historical Association, 1884-1909. *AHR*, v. 15, Oct. 1909: 1-20.

E171. A57, v. 15

[Letter from John Jameson, Butteville, Marion Co., Oregon, to his younger brother, Edwin Jameson, August 17, 1852.] Communicated by J.F.J. Oregon Historical Society, *Quarterly*, v. 10, Dec. 1909: 390-395.

F871.047, v. 10

Preceded by J.F.J.'s letter to the editor, Washington, Nov. 27, 1909. The 1852 letter was written by J.F.J.'s father, and was almost entirely made up of wholesale prices current from his invoice book, from women's shoes packaged (83¢ to $1.00) to preserves per dozen ($1.00).

U. S. Committee on Department Methods. *Message from the President of the United States transmitting a report by the Committee on Department Methods on the documentary historical publications of the United States government, together with a draft of a proposed bill providing for the creation of a permanent Commission on National Historical Publications.* Washington: Government Printing Office. 45 p. (60th Cong., 2d Session, Senate Doc. 714).

1910

Johnson, Edward (1598-1672). *Johnson's Wonderworking Providence, 1628-1651;* edited by J. Franklin Jameson. New York: Scribner, 1910. 285 p. (original narratives of early American history).

F67. J675

Originally published, London 1653 or —4.

The Control of the Higher Education in the United States. Richmond, Ind.: G. O. Ballinger Co., 1910. 27 p. (*The Earlham College Bulletin*, Aug. 1910, v. 7, no. 5.)

LB2341. J3

Address delivered at Earlham College commencement, June 17, 1910.

The Present State of Historical Writing in America. In American Antiquarian Society, Worcester, Mass. *Proceedings*, n.s., v. 20, 1909-1910. p. 408-418.

E172. A35, v. 20

A paper read at the annual meeting of Oct. 19, 1910. Two others on the same topic, by John Bach McMaster and Edward Channing, follow (p. 420-434). J.F.J. dealt particularly with "organized historical work."

Letters of John Bridge [Sept. 9, 1623] and Emmanuel Altham [May 28, 1624]. Edited by J.F.J. Massachusetts Historical Society, *Proceedings*, 1910-11 (Boston, 1911), v. 44: 178-188.

F61. M38, v. 44

Communicated through W. C. Ford at the meeting of Nov. 10, 1910.

Both letters are addressed to James Sherley, Treasurer of the New Plymouth Adventurers, and preserved among the High Court of Admiralty records in the Public Record Office. Bridge was master and Altham captain of the *Little James*, the company's pinnace for Plymouth Colony; Bridge lost his life when it was wrecked in April 1624.

Letter of John Quincy Adams, from Ghent, 1814 [edited by J.F.J.]. *AHR*, v. 15, Apr. 1910: 572-574.

E171. A57, v. 15

Letter of Major-General Johann Kalb, 1777 [edited by J.F.J.]. *AHR*, v. 15, Apr. 1910: 562-567.

E171. A57, v. 15

Letter between the writer and Lafayette.

Letter of the Marquess of Rockingham respecting Defense against John Paul Jones, 1779 [edited by J.F.J.]. *AHR*, v. 15, Apr. 1910: 567-572.

E171. A57, v. 15

Letter of William Henry Trescot on Reconstruction in South Carolina, 1867 [edited by J.F.J.]. *AHR*, v. 15, Apr. 1910: 574-582.

E171. A57, v. 15

Letter of a South Carolinian historian and diplomat.

Letters of Toussaint Louverture and of Edward Stevens, 1798-1800 [edited by J.F.J.]. *AHR*, v. 16, Oct. 1910: 64-101.

E171. A57, v. 16

Letters re the political and diplomatic relations between Louverture, France, and the United States. Stevens was American consul-general in Santo Domingo.

1911

Address to the Daughters of the American Revolution. Memorial Continental Hall, Apr. 19, 1911. *In* Daughters of the American Revolution. *Proceedings of the 20th Continental Congress*, Washington, D. C., Apr. 17-22, 1911. [Washington] 1911. p. 90-93.

E202.5. A164, v. 20

"I am asked to say something to you regarding possible work in history on the part of the National Society. I am glad to respond to such an invitation."

Letters of William T. Barry, 1806-1810, 1829-1831 [edited by J.F.J.]. *AHR*, v. 16, Jan. 1911: 327-336.

E171. A57, v. 16

8 family letters from the first Postmaster-General to be admitted to a seat in the Cabinet.

The First American Discoveries in the Antarctic, 1819 [edited by J.F.J.]. *AHR*, v. 16, July 1911: 794-798.

E171. A57, v. 16

Correspondence chiefly from James Byers of New York, ship-owner, who sent out ships for the purpose of discovery.

Senator Few on the Second Session of the First Congress, 1790 [edited by J.F.J.]. *AHR*, v. 16, July 1911: 789-790.

E171. A57, v. 16

Records of the Settlers at the Head of the French Broad River, 1793-1803 [edited by J.F.J.]. *AHR*, v. 16, July 1911: 791-794.

E171. A57, v. 16

Records showing how "frontier American communities have spontaneously generated. . . ."

1912

Introduction to Gertrude Selwyn Kimball's *Providence in Colonial Times*. Boston: Houghton Mifflin, 1912. p. xv-xxi.

F89. P9K49

Sketch of the life and historical contributions of the author (1863-1910).

Debates on the Declaratory Act and the Repeal of the Stamp Act [Feb. 3 and Mar. 11] 1766, contributed by Charles H. Hull and Harold W. V. Temperley. *AHR*, v. 17, April 1912: 563-586.

E171. A56, v. 17

The introductory note, p. 563-565, is by J.F.J.; it calls attention to the project of the Department of Historical Research for a compilation of all debates of British parliaments on American affairs, and gives the legislative history of the two acts. He also expanded the many abbreviations in the 2nd Earl Hardwicke's ms. published by Temperley; whether he also contributed the numerous annotations to the first text does not appear.

Journal of William K. Beall, July-August, 1812 [edited by J.F.J.]. *AHR*, v. 17, July 1912: 783-808.

E171. A56, v. 17

Journal of an army officer concerning Gen. William Hull's "mismanaged and disastrous campaign."

Diary of Thomas Ewing, August and September, 1841 [edited by J.F.J.]. *AHR*, v. 18, Oct. 1912: 97-112.

E171. A57, v. 18

Diary chiefly concerned with the "serious difference between the President" and his party regarding the rechartering the Bank of the United States.

1913

Danckaerts, Jasper (b. 1639) *Journal, 1679-1680;* edited by Bartlett Burleigh James and J. Franklin Jameson. New York: Scribner, 1913. xxi, 313 p.

E162. D18

"The present edition is substantially that of Mr. Henry C. Murphy, as presented in his edition of 1867."

The Future Uses of History. *History Teacher's Magazine*, v. 4, Feb. 1913: 35-40.

D16.3.S65, v. 4

Originally delivered before the Trustees of the Carnegie Institution of Washington, Dec. 12, 1912. *The History Teacher's Magazine*, after a period as *The Historical Outlook*, was eventually renamed *The Social Studies*, and is so catalogued by the Library of Congress and other libraries. This article was reprinted, with some omissions and minor editorial changes, in *AHR*, v. 65, Oct. 1959: 61-77.

The International Congress of Historical Studies held at London. *AHR*, v. 18, July 1913: 679-691.

E171. A56, v. 18

The 4th Congress of April 1913, arranged by the British Academy.

Notes of Colonel W[illiam] G. Moore, private secretary to President Johnson, 1866-1868, contributed by St. George L. Sioussat. *AHR*, v. 19, Oct. 1913: 98-132.

E171. A56, v. 19

The annotations supplied by J.F.J., with some help from Sioussat.

Correspondence of the Russian Ministers in Washington, 1818-1825, I [edited by J.F.J.]. *AHR*, v. 18, Jan. 1913: 309-345. ————, II [edited by J.F.J.]. *AHR*, v. 18, Apr. 1913: 537-562.

E171. A57, v. 18

Letters re Russia's policy regarding Spanish-American colonies and affairs of the Russian-American Co.

1914

The History of Historical Societies; address by Dr. J. Franklin Jameson at the seventy-fifth anniversary of the Georgia Historical Society. Savannah, Ga., *Morning News* print. Cover-title, 19 p.

Typical Steps of American Expansion. *History Teacher's Magazine*, v. 5, Feb. 1914: [39]-43.

Read at the International Congress of Historical Studies, "in the hall of the Royal Society in Burlington House," London, Apr. 3, 1913. Its genesis is described in J.F.J. to H.W.V. Temperley, May 7, 1912, Donnan and Stock, p. 149-150.

WAH 14: 447

The Need of a National Archive Building. American Library Association, *Bulletin*, v. 8, July 1914: 130-136.

Z673. A5B6, v. 8

"Present conditions interpose almost intolerable obstacles to the progress of history." Followed by comments by Gaillard Hunt and Victor H. Paltsits.

1914: 63

Journal of Jean Baptiste Truteau on the Upper Missouri, "Primiere Partie," June 7, 1794-March 26, 1795 [edited by J.F.J.]. *AHR*, v. 19, Jan. 1914: 299-333.

E171. A57, v. 19

The journal relates "to the history of exploration of the Upper Missouri."

Estimates of the Value of Slaves, 1815 [edited by J.F.J.]. *AHR*, v. 19, July 1914: 813-838.

E171. A57, v. 19

From the papers of the arbitration commission under Article I of the Treaty of Ghent.

Letters relating to the Negotiations at Ghent, 1812-1814 [edited by J.F.J.]. *AHR*, v. 20, Oct. 1914: 108-129.

E171. A57, v. 20

1915

The Age of Erudition. *In Representative Phi Beta Kappa Orations* [1837-1910], edited for the United Chapters of Phi Beta Kappa by Clark S. Northrup, William C. Lane [and] John C. Schwab. Boston: Houghton Mifflin, 1915. p. 326-343.

PS663. PSN6

Delivered before Phi Beta Kappa of Illinois, at the University of Chicago, June 12, 1905. Deals with European scholarship, 1650-1750, and especially with the work of Mabillon and the Bollandists. The volume was reissued in 1930 (New York: Elisha Parnele Press).

American Historical Review. An historical statement concerning *The American Historical Review.* Washington, *AHR*, 1915. 8 p.

Signed by J.F.J. along with 5 other members of the board of editorials: Carl Becker, George L. Burr, Edward P. Cheyney, James H. Robinson, and Frederick J. Turner.

WAH 15:93

The Meeting of the American Historical Association in Chicago. *AHR*, v. 20, Apr. 1915: 503-527.

E171. A57, v. 20

The Meeting of the American Historical Association in California. *AHR*, v. 21, Oct. 1915: 1-11.

E171. A57, v. 21

Letters from Lafayette to Luzerne, 1780-1782, I [edited by J.F.J.]. *AHR*, v. 20, Jan. 1915: 341-376. ————————, II [edited by J.F.J.]. *AHR*, v. 20, Apr. 1915: 577-612.

E171. A57, v. 20

1915-16

Bancroft, Frederic, John H. Latané and Dunbar Rowland. Why the American Historical Association Needs Thorough Reorganization. Washington: National Capital Press, 1915 [-16]. 69 p.

E172. A69

Four pamphlets with continuous pagination; the last two, Bancroft's *Misrepresentations and Concealments in opposition to reform in the American Historical Association* (dated at end Dec. 27, 1915), and *Correspondence between Frederick Bancroft and Charles H.*

*Haskins about financial irregularities in the American Historical
Association* (terminating with Oct. 11, 1916) presumably appeared
in 1916. The authors, who also vented their discontents in the
Nation, alleged that an inner ring ran the Association and *Review*
to suit itself, and turned much of their wrath against a *"life member of the Council, member and chairman of the editorial board,
managing editor of the Review, acting secretary and virtually
acting treasurer of the Association* (when his subordinate in Carnegie Institution is in Europe) and *self-chosen spokesmen of the
board, Council and Association."* J.F.J., who was further accused
of helping himself to the Association's funds, commented upon this
onslaught, temperately enough so far as his share in the accusations
was concerned, in several letters between July 9, 1915 and Jan. 4,
1916 published by Donnan and Stock (p. 181-190 *passim*). The
insurgents received no support from the body of the Association.

1916

The Meeting of the American Historical Association at Washington.
  AHR, v. 21, April 1916: 441-467.

                                          E171. A57, v. 21

1917

The Association. AHA, *Annual Report for 1917.* Washington: G.P.O.,
  1920. p. 303-312.

                                          L331. E172. A60
  "The line of descent from the Protestant Association of 1584
to that framed in Philadelphia by the First Continental Congress
143 years ago is entirely clear."

The Meeting of the American Historical Association at Cincinnati.
  AHR, v. 22, Apr. 1917: 509-534.

Historical Scholars in War-time. *AHR,* v. 22, July 1917: 831-835.

Protocols of Conferences of Representatives of the Allied Powers
  respecting Spanish America, 1824-1825 [edited by J.F.J.]. *AHR,*
  v. 22, Apr. 1917: 595-616.

                                          E171. A57, v. 22

Paris in 1870: Letters of Mary Corinna Putnam [edited by J.F.J.].
  AHR, v. 22, July 1917: 836-841.

                                          E171. A57, v. 22
  3 family letters from the first woman graduate of the New York
College of Pharmacy.

Kearsage and Alabama: French Official Report, 1864 [edited by J.F.J.]. *AHR*, v. 23, Oct. 1917: 119-123.

E171. A57, v. 23

1918

In memoriam: Henry Adams. AHA, *Annual Report for 1918*. Washington: G.P.O., 1921. v. 1: 71-72.

E172. A60 1918

Speaking for the Executive Council of the AHA, concerning its president in 1893-94.

A New Historical Journal. *Hispanic American Historical Review*, v. 1, Feb. 1918: 2-7.

F1401. H66, v. 1

After a letter from President Woodrow Wilson on page 1, the dean of the profession and editor of the *AHR* discourses on the proliferation of historical periodicals, local and specialized; of the latter, three had preceded the *Hispanic American* (the *Catholic Historical Review*, the *Military Historian and Economist*—which expired this same year—and the *Journal of Negro History*).

The American Minister in Berlin, on the Revolution of March, 1848 [edited by J.F.J.]. *AHR*, v. 23, Jan. 1918: 355-373.

E171. A57, v. 23

The Confederacy and the Declaration of Paris [edited by J.F.J.]. *AHR*, v. 23, July 1918: 826-835.

E171. A57, v. 23

Documents taken from the papers of William Henry Trescot, Assistant Secretary of State under President Buchanan.

The River Plate Voyages, 1798-1800 [note appended by J.F.J.]. *AHR*, v. 23, July 1918: 816-825.

E171. A57, v. 23

1919

[The archives of] the United States of America. Communicated by J. Franklin Jameson, Ph.D., corresponding Fellow of the Royal Historical Society [etc.]. *In* British and Allied archives during the war [intro. and 8 parts]. Royal Historical Society, *Transactions*, 4th series, v. 2 [p. 20-58]. p. 37-40.

DA20. R9, 4th Ser., v. 2

London, 1919

Amherst petition on the embargo [Aug. 30] 1808. Massachusetts Historical Society, *Proceedings*, 1918-19 (Boston, 1919), v. 52: 161-163.

F61. M38, v. 52

At the meeting of Mar. 13, 1919, the editor, W. C. Ford, reported J.F.J.'s gift of a contemporary copy certified by the town clerk (p. 140).

Diary and Memoranda of William L. Marcy, 1849-1851 [note appended by J.F.J.]. *AHR*, v. 24, Apr. 1919: 444-462.

E171. A57, v. 24

Papers of a secretary of war and later secretary of state.

Diary and Memoranda of William L. Marcy, 1857 [edited by J.F.J.]. *AHR*, v. 24, July 1919: 641-653.

E171. A57, v. 24

1920

The Meeting of the American Historical Association at Cleveland. *AHR*, v. 25, April 1920: 369-390.

E171. A57, v. 25

The American Council of Learned Societies. *AHR*, v. 25, Apr. 1920: 440-446.

E171. A57, v. 25

The American Historical Review, 1895-1920. *AHR*, v. 26, Oct. 1920: 1-17.

E171. A57, v. 26

J.F.J. was the first editor, 1895-1901, and resumed the editorship during 1905-28. This is his account of its background and genesis, and a brief summary through the first 25 volumes.

John Clark [mate] of the *Mayflower*. Massachusetts Historical Society, *Proceedings*, 1920-21 (Boston, 1922), v. 54: 61-76.

F61. M38, v. 54

Presented at the meeting of Nov. 11, 1920.

12 documents, all but one from the archives of the Indies at Seville, relating to Clark's capture off Virginia, June 1611, and imprisonment in Havana and Madrid, 1611-1616.

The Arrival of the Pilgrims. A lecture delivered at Brown University, Providence, R. I., November 21, 1920. [Providence] Printed by the University, 1920. 40 p.

F68. J3

Delivered on the 300th anniversary of the landing of the Pilgrims in Provincetown harbor.

Henry Adams and Garibaldi, 1860 [edited by J.F.J.]. *AHR*, v. 25, Jan. 1920: 241-255.

E171. A57, v. 25

Letters by Adams relating Garibaldi's campaign.

Spanish Policy toward Virginia, 1606-1612; Jamestown, Ecija, and John Clark of the Mayflower [edited by J.F.J.]. *AHR*, v. 25, Apr. 1920: 448-479.

E171. A57, v. 25

Letter of Daniel Webster, 1833 [edited by J.F.J.]. *AHR*, v. 25, July 1920: 695-697.

E171. A57, v. 25

Letter to Stephen White, a member of the Massachusetts Senate.

Letter of William Wirt, 1819 [edited by J.F.J.]. *AHR*, v. 25, July 1920: 692-695.

E171. A57, v. 25

Letter of attorney-general of the United States to John Coalter, a judge of the Virginia Supreme Court of Appeals.

1921

The [35th] Meeting of the American Historical Association at Washington [Dec. 28-30, 1920]. *AHR*, v. 26, Apr. 1921: 413-439.

E171. A57, v. 26

Review of Michael J. O'Brien's *A Hidden Phase of American History: Ireland's Part in America's Struggle for Liberty* (New York: Dodd, Mead, 1920). *AHR*, v. 26, July 1921: 797-799.

E171. A57, v. 26

The Anglo-American Conference of Professors of History. *AHR*, v. 27, Oct. 1921: 58-63.

E171. A57, v. 27

On the occasion of the opening of the Institute of Historical Research at the University of London, July 11-16, 1921.

General M. C. Meigs on the Conduct of the Civil War [edited by J.F.J.]. *AHR*, v. 26, Jan. 1921: 285-303.

E171. A57, v. 26

Journal of a French Traveller in the Colonies, 1765, I [edited by J.F.J.]. *AHR*, v. 26, July 1921: 726-747.
——————, II [edited by J.F.J.]. *AHR*, v. 27, Oct. 1921: 70-89.

E171. A57, v. 27

Journal of as yet an unidentified Frenchman.

1922

The Meeting of the American Historical Association at St. Louis. *AHR*, v. 27, Apr. 1922: 405-425.

Washington in 1834; Letter of Robert C. Caldwell [edited by J.F.J.]. *AHR*, v. 27, Jan. 1922: 271-281.

E171. A57, v. 27

Letter of a Marine Corps lieutenant to his father.

Lord Sackville's Papers respecting Virginia, 1613-1631, I [edited by J.F.J.]. *AHR*, v. 27, Apr. 1922: 493-538.
——————, II [edited by J.F.J.]. *AHR*, v. 27, July 1922: 738-765.

E171. A57, v. 27

1923

The American Historian's Raw Materials, an address by J. Franklin Jameson . . . with the presentation and other exercises at the dedication of the William L. Clements Library of Americana, June 15, 1923. Ann Arbor: University of Michigan, 1923. 63 p.

E175. J312

J.F.J.'s address was also issued separately: *The American Historian's Raw Materials*, an address at the dedication of the William L. Clements Library of Americana, June 15, 1923, by J. Franklin Jameson, with the same pagination, 25-50.

An Historian's Raw Materials

Also published in *Michigan History Magazine*, v. 8, Apr. 1924: 107-125.

Privateering and Piracy in the Colonial Period: illustrative documents, edited under the auspices of the National Society of the Colonial Dames of America, by J.F.J. New York: Macmillan, 1923. xxvi, 619 p.

E195. J32

Privateering and Piracy

Reviewed by Charles M. Andrews in *AHR*, v. 29, Apr. 1924: 564-565.

E171. A57, v. 29

AHR, Apr. 1924: 564-565.
American Journal of International Law, v. 28, July 1924: 643-644.
Canadian Historical Review, v. 5, Sept. 1924: 270-271.

The University Centre for Research in Washington. *AHR*, v. 28, Jan. 1923: 259-262.

E171. A57, v. 28

The Meeting of the American Historical Association at New Haven. *AHR*, v. 28, Apr. 1923: 417-439.

E171. A57, v. 28

A Pure History Law. *AHR*, v. 28, July 1923: 699-701.

E171. A57, v. 28

The Wisconsin law of 1923.

Letters of Robert Biddulph, 1779-1783. *AHR*, v. 29, Oct. 1923: 87-109. Introduction by Hon. Violet Biddulph; annotations by J.F.J.

E171. A57, v. 29

Masson, Marjorie, *and* J.F.J. The Odyssey of Thomas Muir. *AHR*, v. 29, Oct. 1923: 49-72.

E171. A57, v. 29

Muir, convicted of sedition in Scotland in 1793 and transported to Australia the next year, escaped to North America in 1796 and ended up in France, where he died in 1799. J.F.J. amplified the part relating to Muir's adventures in America, and Miss Masson of the University of Victoria insisted on his being included in the authorship.

1924

Henry W. Hilliard to James Buchanan, 1858 [edited by J.F.J.]. *AHR*, v. 29, Apr. 1924: 513.

E171. A57, v. 29

The writer was an Alabama politician.

W. E. Gladstone to Sir Frederick Bruce, 1866 [edited by J.F.J.]. *AHR*, v. 29, Apr. 1924: 517-518.

E171. A57, v. 29

Letter to British minister in Washington relating to public finance.

The Meeting of the American Historical Association at Columbus. *AHR*, v. 29, Apr. 1924: 423-448.

E171. A57, v. 29

On the Journals of the House of Representatives, 1836 [edited by J.F.J.]. *AHR*, v. 29, Apr. 1924: 510-512.

E171. A57, v. 29

Two letters to James K. Polk, Speaker of the House of Representatives, 24th Congress.

Papers of Count Tisza, 1914-1918 [edited by J.F.J.]. *AHR*, v. 29, Jan. 1924: 301-315.

Note: Papers of Count Tisza [edited by J.F.J.]. *AHR*, v. 29, Apr. 1924: 522.

E171. A57, v. 29

Papers of the Hungarian prime minister.

William Lattimore to his Constituents, 1805 [edited by J.F.J.]. *AHR*, v. 29, Apr. 1924: 506-510.

E171. A57, v. 29

Lattimore was territorial delegate from Mississippi in the 8th and 9th Congresses.

The Assassination of President Lincoln, 1865 [edited by J.F.J.]. *AHR*, v. 29, Apr. 1924: 514-517.

E171. A57, v. 29

Letter of James Tanner, a clerk in the War Department, to a friend.

Marbois on the Fur Trade, 1784 [edited by J.F.J.]. *AHR*, v. 29, July 1924: 725-740.

E171. A57, v. 29

Documents of French chargé d'affaires in the United States to French minister of foreign affairs resulting from Marbois' participation with Lafayette in the negotiations with the Six Nations.

1925

The Meeting of the American Historical Association at Richmond. *AHR*, v. 30, Apr. 1925: 451-477.

E171. A57, v. 30

Autobiography of Omar ibn Said, slave in North Carolina, 1831 [edited by J.F.J.]. *AHR*, v. 30, July 1925: 787-795.

E171. A57, v. 30

A remarkable document, from an Arabic ms. lent to J.F.J. by Howland Wood of New York, Curator of the American Numismatic Society. Omar was a Fila of the Kingdom of Futa, now in French Senegal; they were of mixed Berber and Negro stock, of Mohammedan faith, and of Arabic speech and writing. Born about 1770, he was captured in a raid and brought to Charleston in 1807. Shortly before the slave trade became illegal, he ran off to Fayetteville, N. C., was acquired by James Owen and kept in comfort on his plantation in Bladen County, where he lived until after the Civil War. This Arabic ms. was sent to New York City in 1836 and came into the possession of Theodore Dwight. He had two translations made, the better of which, by the Rev. Isaac Bird, is given here, slightly revised by Dr. F. M. Moussan, Secretary of the Egyptian Legation in Washington. Annotations by J.F.J.

From the Autobiography of Herschel V. Johnson, 1856-1867 [edited by J.F.J.]. *AHR*, v. 30, Jan. 1925: 311-336.

E171. A57, v. 30

The writer was prominent in Georgian politics.

The Escape of Louis Philippe, 1848 [edited by J.F.J.]. *AHR*, v. 30, Apr. 1925: 556-560.

E171. A57, v. 30

2 letters of the American vice-consul at Havre.

Talleyrand and Jaudenes, 1795 [edited by J.F.J.]. *AHR*, v. 30, July 1925: 778-787.

E171. A57, v. 30

Documents from Josef de Jaudenes, the Spanish envoy to the United States, to Godoy, his minister of foreign affairs.

1926

The Meeting of the American Historical Association at Ann Arbor. *AHR*, v. 31, Apr. 1926: 415-442.

E171. A57, v. 31

The American Revolution Considered as a Social Movement. Princeton: Princeton University Press, 1926. 1951.

E209. J33

Lectures delivered in Nov. 1925 on the Louis Clark Vanuxem Foundation.

Reprinted by photographic process. New York: Peter Smith, 1950.

Reissued as a paperback by the Beacon Press of Boston [1956].

American Revolution as a Social Movement.

Reprinted in 1940. 100 p.

Despatches of Castelnau de la Mauvissiere (on Frobisher, Gilbert, de la Roche, Drake), 1577-1581 [edited by J.F.J.]. *AHR*, v. 31, Jan. 1926: 285-296.

E171. A57, v. 31

A Confederate Private at Fort Donelson, 1862 [edited by J.F.J.]. *AHR*, v. 31, Apr. 1926: 477-484.

E171. A57, v. 31

1927

A Possible Enrichment of the Teaching of History. *Amherst Graduates' Quarterly*, v. 16, Feb. 1927: 67-79.

LH1. A5G7, v. 16

This and the other three articles by Ramsay Muir (Univ. of Manchester), Edward P. Cheyney, and Laurence B. Packard, constituted a symposium on the study and teaching of history, delivered before the Alumni Council the previous November. J.F.J. sought enrichment "by an ample inclusion of the history of civilization." "Let the historical professor put forth all the powers of his mind to deal with all that history in its broadest interpretation can include."

The Meeting of the American Historical Association at Rochester. *AHR*, v. 32, Apr. 1927: 429-454.

E171. A57, v. 32

A briefer version appeared in the *Bulletin* of the International Committee of Historical Sciences, v. 1, pt. 2, June 1927: 259-262.

Introduction to a bibliography of the history of the United States. International Committee of Historical Sciences, *Bulletin*, v. 1, pt. 2, June 1927: 226-229.

D3. A17, v. 1

43 unnumbered entries under the headings: General, Bibliographies in general histories; Special bibliographies; Manuscripts; Periodicals and serials. What we should now call a "basic" list.

Major-General Henry Lee and Lieutenant-General Sir George Beckwith on Peace in 1813 [edited by J.F.J.]. *AHR*, v. 32, Jan. 1927: 284-292.

E171. A57, v. 32

Despatches from the United States Consulate in New Orleans, 1801-1803, I [edited by J.F.J.]. *AHR*, v. 32, July 1927: 801-824.
──────────, II [edited by J.F.J.]. *AHR*, v. 33, Jan. 1928: 331-359.

E171. A57, v. 32 & 33

Letters relating chiefly to trade involving Spanish and Louisiana vessels.

1928

A provisional list of printed lists of ambassadors and other diplomatic representatives. International Committee of Historical Sciences, *Bulletin*, v. 1, pt. 4, Mar. 1928: 475-490.

D3. A17, v. 1

i. Generalities; ii. Foreign powers to some countries; iii-xxiv [Countries alphabetically, Austria to Venice]. J.F.J. also contributed, in this issue, to an "Enquête sur les atles historiques en preparation," a note of about a page (p. 511-512): "Etats unis d'Amerique. Atlas of the Historical Geography of the United States." This was the Carnegie Institution project which only reached publication in 1932, under the editorship of C. O. Paullin.

Review of *Histoire et historiens depuis cinquente ans* (Paris: Alcan, 1927. 2 v. Bibliotheque de la Revue historique [founded in 1876]). *AHR*, v. 34, Oct. 1928: 92-93.

E171. A57, v. 34

The Meeting of the American Historical Association at Washington. *AHR*, v. 33, Apr. 1928: 517-543.

E171. A57, v. 33

Letters of a West Pointer, 1860-1861 [edited by J.F.J.]. *AHR*, v. 33, Apr. 1928: 599-617.

E171. A57, v. 33

19 letters of a Confederate officer.

Jefferson to William Short on Mr. and Mrs. Merry, 1804 [edited by J.F.J.]. *AHR*, v. 33, July 1928: 832-835.

E171. A57, v. 33

Letter to American diplomatist regarding official etiquette in relation to the British minister and his wife.

Henry J. Raymond on the Republican Caucuses of July, 1866 [edited by J.F.J.]. *AHR*, v. 33, July 1928: 835-842.

E171. A57, v. 33

1929

The International Historical Congress at Oslo. *AHR*, v. 34, Jan. 1929: 265-273.

E171. A57, v. 34

The 6th International Congress of Historical Sciences, Aug. 14-18, 1928.

1929-1937

Annual Reports of the Chief, Division of Manuscripts.

Appear in the *Annual Report of the Librarian of Congress* (Washington: U. S. Government Printing Office, 1929-37 Z663. A2) as follows:

1929 p. 45-75
1930 p. 61-94

1931   p. 53-86
1932   p. 33-60
1933   p. 25-40
1934   p. 32-45
1935   p. 30-45
1936   p. 30-45
1937   p. 30-40

1930

Ephraim Douglass Adams. AHA, *Annual Report for 1930* (Washington: U. S. Govt. Printing Office, 1931), v. 1: 48-49.

E172. A60 1930, v. 1

Professor Adams of Stanford University (b. 1865), by dying on Sept. 1, 1930, had missed elevation to the presidency of the AHA.

Notes from the Archives of Scotland concerning America. American Historical Association, *Annual Report for 1930* (Washington: U.S.G.P.O., 1931), v. 1: 97-122.

E172. A60 1930, v. 1

Mostly "decreets" of the High Court of Admiralty, 1703-1788, supplemented by a few records of the Criminal Court of Admiralty, 1720-84, and the Court of Sessions, 1773-74, all preserved at the General Register House, Edinburgh. J.F.J. had made the preliminary reconnaissance in the Spring of 1913.

The London Expenditures of the Confederate Secret Service [edited by J.F.J.]. *AHR*, v. 35, July 1930: 811-824.

E171. A57, v. 35

Dispatch from Henry Holze, Confederate commercial agent in London, to Secretary Judah P. Benjamin, Dec. 31, 1864, with enclosed accounts from Nov. 14, 1861.

1931

Introduction. *In Persecution and Liberty; essays in honor of George Lincoln Burr*. New York: Century Co., 1931 (xviii, 482 p.). p. xv-xviii.

D6. P4

J.F.J.'s association with Burr went back to the AHA meeting of 1890.

Review of James Truslow Adams's *The Adams Family* (Boston: Little, Brown, 1930). *AHR*, v. 36, Jan. 1931: 410-412.

E171. A57, v. 36

1932

Introduction. *In Historical Scholarship in America: Needs and Opportunities;* a report by the Committee of the American Historical Association on the Planning of Research, A.M. Schlesinger, Chairman. New York: R. Long & R. R. Smith, 1932 [ix, 146 p.], p. 3-11.
D13. A6

Introductory preface. *In* Clemence, Stella R. (ed.), *The Harkness collection in the Library of Congress.* Calendar of Spanish manuscripts concerning Peru, 1531-1651. Washington: G.P.O., 1942.
Z16621. U58 H3

1933

Johnson, Allen (Jan. 29, 1870-Jan. 18, 1931). *In Dictionary of American Biography,* edited by Dumas Malone. v. 10: 79-81.
E176. D56, v. 10

Life of the first editor of the *DAB,* by the Chairman of the Committee of Management.

1934

Early Days of the American Historical Association, 1884-1895. *AHR,* v. 40, Oct. 1934: 1-9.
E171. A57, v. 40

1935

Edward Potts Cheyney as a Member of the American Historical Association. *In* Lingelbach, William E., ed. *Portrait of a Historian, Edward Potts Cheyney.* Philadelphia: University of Pennsylvania Press, 1935.

Notice of Beckles Willson's *Friendly Relations: a Narrative of Britain's Ministers and Ambassadors to America, 1791-1930* (Boston: Little, Brown, 1934). *AHR,* v. 40, Apr. 1935: 557-559.
E171. A57, v. 40

Annihilation in a temperate paragraph.

Notice of Claude Moore Fuess's *Amherst: the Story of a New England College* (Boston: Little, Brown, 1935). *AHR,* v. 41, Oct. 1935: 197.
E171. A57, v. 41

Amherst as preserver of the standards of "pre-Hibernian Massachusetts."

1938

John Franklin Jameson. *AHR*, v. 43, Jan. 1938: 243-252.

E171. A57, v. 43

Obituary memoir with portrait.

Cheyney, Edward P.

American Council of Learned Societies, Bulletin, no. 27.

1940

Items from the library of Dr. J. Franklin Jameson, deceased. L. F. Stock, trustee, estate of Dr. J. F. Jameson, 1017 Michigan Ave., N.E., Washington, D. C. [Ann Arbor, Mich.: Edwards Bros., 1940]. unpaged.

Z997. J33

1671 entries, 219 "reports, etc." Each part in alphabetical order.

1945

Some Bryce-Jameson correspondence. Edited by Leo Francis Stock. *AHR*, v. 50, Jan. 1945: 261-298.

E171. A57, v. 50

17 letters from J.F.J. to James Bryce, Viscount Bryce, and 7 from Bryce to J.F.J., 1907-21; 2 between J.F.J. and Lady Bryce after Lord Bryce's death in 1922; all from the files of the Division of Historical Research, Carnegie Institution of Washington.

1948

Senator [Albert J.] Beveridge, J. Franklin Jameson, and John Marshall. Edited by Elizabeth Donnan and Leo F. Stock. *MVHR*, v. 35, Dec. 1948: 463-492.

F351. M66, v. 35

33 letters exchanged by Beveridge and Jameson, June 7, 1913-Nov. 19, 1919, concerning the former's life of John Marshall, with a 4-page introductory note.

1949

Senator [Albert J.] Beveridge, J. Franklin Jameson, and Abraham Lincoln. Edited by Elizabeth Donnan and Leo F. Stock. *MVHR*, v. 35, Mar. 1949: 639-673.

F351. M66, v. 35

38 letters between Beveridge and Jameson, Feb. 28, 1923-Jan.

17, 1927, while the former was at work upon his unpublished life of Lincoln, with a 2-page introductory note.

Shelley, Fred. The Interest of J. Franklin Jameson in the National Archives, 1908-1934. *American Archivist,* v. 12, April 1949: 99-130.
CD3020. A45, v. 12

1956

An Historian's World; Selections from the Correspondence of John Franklin Jameson. Edited by Elizabeth Donnan and Leo F. Stock. Philadelphia: American Philosophical Society, 1956. 382 p. (Memoirs of the American Philosophical Society, v. 42.)
D15. J27A4

Some 500 letters, 1880-1937.

1958

Leland, Waldo Gifford. Jameson, John Franklin (Sept. 19, 1859-Sept. 28, 1937). *In Dictionary of American Biography,* v. 22, Supplement Two. New York: Scribner, 1958. p. 339-344.
E176. D56, v. 22

DATE DUE